OUNCE OF PREVENTION

Ounce of Prevention

❦

Divorce-Proofing
Your Marriage

GARY RICHMOND
AND LISA C. BODE

VINE
BOOKS

Servant Publications
Ann Arbor, Michigan

Vine Books is an imprint of Servant Publications especially designed to serve Evangelical Christians.

The case histories in this book are true, but the names and identifying details have been changed to protect the identities of the individuals involved unless otherwise indicated. In some cases, the stories are compilations designed to address the issues without identifying the actual people.

All Scripture quotations, unless otherwise indicated, are from THE HOLY BIBLE: NEW INTERNATIONAL VERSION. © 1973, 1978, 1983 International Bible Society. Used by permission of Zondervan Publishing House. All rights reserved. The "NIV" and "New International Version" trademarks are registered in the United States Patent and Trademark Office by International Bible Society.

Verses marked RSV are from the Revised Standard Version of the Bible, copyrighted 1946, 1952, 1971 by the Division of Christian Education of the National Council of Churches of Christ in the USA. All rights reserved. Selected texts have been taken from the Living Bible (LB), © 1971, owned by assignment by KNT Charitable Trust, and the New King James Version of the Bible (NKJV), © 1979, 1980, 1982 by Thomas Nelson, Inc., Publishers. All rights reserved.

Published by Servant Publications
P.O. Box 8617
Ann Arbor, Michigan 48107

95 96 97 98 99 10 9 8 7 6 5 4 3 2 1

Printed in the United States of America
ISBN 0-89283-804-3

Library of Congress Cataloging-in-Publication Data

Richmond, Gary
   Ounce of prevention : divorce-proofing your marriage /
Gary Richmond and Lisa C. Bode.
     p. cm.
   ISBN 0-89283-804-3
   1. Marriage—Religious aspects—Christianity. 2.
Married people—Religious life. I. Bode, Lisa C. II.
Title.
BV835.R54   1995
248.8'44—dc20   95-12292
                                   CIP

Dedications

Lisa:
With love and appreciation this book is dedicated to my husband, Tom—my lifetime partner and devoted friend.

Gary:
This book is dedicated to my beloved wife, Carol, and to our dear friends, Dick and Naomi Landorf.

Contents

A Word to the Wise

According to a recent study of U.S. census records, the chances are two out of three that your marriage will end in divorce. Divorce, for most people, looks something like this:

- Exchanging your children with your mate every other weekend

- Divided finances, dragging you near the poverty line

- $18,000 out of your estate to pay legal expenses

- Loss of half of your friends, who will no longer feel comfortable with you as a single in their married world

- Your children becoming more prone to suicide, drugs, and promiscuity

Are you concerned about these statistics? We are! They concern us enough to make us write this book—to expose the many "predators" that can rip a marriage to shreds, leaving the partners emotionally devastated, financially destitute, and very disillusioned.

Love is not sweeter the second time around. So say the statistics. A 67 percent failure rate for first marriages quickly ascends to a 75 percent failure rate for second marriages and 84 percent for third marriages. We do not learn by our mistakes in marriage; we repeat them. The best chance we will ever have for our happiness and the happiness of our children is to make our present marriage work.

There are dozens of predators that stalk a marriage, with no less intensity than a lion stalks its helpless prey. Before we know it, we are hapless victims, asking ourselves, "How did this ever happen?"

Divorce doesn't have to happen to you or to anyone. Benjamin Franklin said, "An ounce of prevention is worth a pound of cure." In the case of marriage, an ounce of prevention means learning how to identify the predators, and knowing what to do when we catch even a glimpse of one in our marriage.

What predators are we talking about? What predators can steal our affection, respect, and love? There are dozens of them. *Adultery. Physical abuse. Verbal abuse. Unusual and unhealthy control. Unfulfilled expectations. Money. Lies.*

We want to equip our readers in two ways: First, we want to help you identify and understand the predators you may be facing. Second, we want to show you clear and practical ways to overcome those predators.

We must warn you that some of the predators are so deadly that nothing we could say in this book can help you survive their onslaught. In those few cases, we will offer direction that will lead you to safety.

Both Gary, through his pastoral ministry, and Lisa,* in her private counseling practice, have worked for more than a decade with a steady stream of people who desperately reach out to them for help. The need for marital counseling is so great in our churches and communities that, though our schedules have been full to the brim, we feel we have not even scratched the surface. There is a call for help. We want to answer the call. We want to make available to you as much as we can of the knowledge we would offer if we could meet face-to-face with you.

---

* Occurrences of the names Gary and Lisa in this book always refer to the coauthors. All other names and identifying details in case studies have been changed unless stated otherwise.

We want to reveal the ravages of the predators that have attacked so many husbands and wives, who wanted the best that marriage could offer but had to face the worst. We want to pass on what we have learned from courageous and committed couples who have fought off the predators and built stronger marriages. We also want you to benefit from the examples of those strong marriages we have known.

Marriage is a priority. When given its rightful place, the jungle turns into a beautiful garden. We will journey with you through the importance of making truth, partnership, integrity, and romance a high priority in your marriage. We both strongly believe that marriage is for a lifetime. Gary and Carol have shared thirty-one years of marriage; Lisa and Tom have shared eleven. We agree that our marriages are the most important relationships in our lives, next to our relationship with God. We are both devoted to building our marriages, guarding ourselves against the predators, and dealing with them when they appear.

If you are hurting in your marriage, we want to encourage you. This book was written to give you the hope and insight you need to make a positive difference in your relationship. Our hope and prayer is that you will benefit greatly from what is offered in these pages.

> "For I know the plans I have for you," declares the Lord, "plans to prosper you and not to harm you, plans to give you hope and a future."
>
> **Jeremiah 29:11**

ONE

Great Expectations...
No Expectations

Thirty-one years ago, Carol and Gary stood at the altar in a softly lit sanctuary. They were in love and had so many stars in their eyes it's a wonder they didn't get burned! It was a wonderful wedding, and they both still believe it was as good as weddings get. They made sacred promises to love and cherish and honor each other for the rest of their lives, through joy and sorrow, in sickness and in health, in plenty and in want. As sincere as they both were, neither of them had a clue as to how the negatives of the marriage vows—sorrow and sickness and want—would affect their relationship. Neither did they know how very difficult it would be at times to honor and cherish each other.

Most of what Carol and Gary brought to the altar that day were simply expectations. Then, with less than an hour of premarital counseling, they were pronounced husband and wife and set loose in a world filled with predators that could destroy their marriage.

Their only weapon against the onslaughts on their marriage was their character. They were committed to keeping their word, making adjustments and compromising for the sake of their marriage. While their character held their marriage together, they would have been spared a lot of sorrow if they'd had some other weapons. Their commitment and character ensured the duration of their marriage, but not its quality.

Just weeks before he left to fight in Vietnam, Gary's brother Steve, a newly trained Marine, had joked, "Watch out for me, man. I've had eight hours of training in hand-to-hand combat." Gary had caught his meaning in a second. In not too many days he could be locked in a life-and-death struggle—with only eight hours of training. That's just a day at work, a day in class. It wasn't enough; he knew it and Gary knew it, and neither he nor Gary felt good about it.

The one hour of premarital counseling Carol and Gary received wasn't enough counseling for a marriage. Eight hours would not have been enough either. It is very hard to prepare for a one-time journey when you have never seen the trail and aren't sure of the destination.

Marriage is by far the most important human relationship. It is far more complex than Gary or Carol could have ever imagined. It has more bearing on personal happiness and fulfillment than the sum total of career, friendships, and all the other ways people spend their time. And yet Gary and Carol left the church that wonderful night married, but in ignorant bliss.

What happened after that day was influenced by the expectations they both brought to their marriage. They had never explored each other's expectations, so they experienced a lot of surprises. They were shocked by their discoveries.

Gary came from what has come to be called a dysfunctional family. His father and mother, both of whom had a history of alcoholism, met in a bar just after each had experienced being dumped from very short-term marriages. His father's first marriage had lasted for about two weeks and his mother's just short of a year. Then they married each other—before either had healed from the pain of their first marriage, or had dealt with their obsessive behaviors.

Gary's father quit drinking when Gary's older brother was born, but his mother did not quit. She remained alcoholic and became addicted to prescription drugs, an addiction that lasted until her death at age fifty-seven.

Gary's father's parents divorced—in the days when you "just didn't do such a thing." His father ran away and saw neither of his parents for years, but was eventually reunited with his mother (also an alcoholic) and had a loving relationship with her until she died.

Gary's mother was raised by a wonderful mother, but her real father was killed in the First World War. Her mother remarried and Gary's mother never felt close to her alcoholic stepfather. He was a colorful man, a professional baseball player who had played against the great Babe Ruth; but he was unfaithful throughout the duration of the marriage. He was still chasing women in bars into his eighties.

None of the men in Gary's family were openly affectionate with women—and certainly not with men. Touching another man was considered inappropriate, except for a manly slap on the back or a vigorous handshake. The women in Gary's family wanted to show him affection, but Gary, trying to preserve his developing idea of manhood, recoiled from their attempts. Gary liked their affection but was uncomfortable receiving it. His family didn't talk about such things.

On the other hand, Carol's family was right out of "Ozzie and Harriet," "Father Knows Best," or "Leave It to Beaver." Her parents were respectable, responsible, devoted church members who did everything together. They were well connected with their extended families, affectionate, enjoyed family traditions and vacations, and had no obsessive behaviors. Both of her brothers were Eagle Scouts, and her father was the scoutmaster. All the children were well-behaved, had monitored responsibilities, and had lots of friends. They were active in school functions as well as church. The worst thing that could be said about the family was that it was too military or rigid. But it looked ideal to Gary, and as he and Carol dated, he hoped their future family would be as wholesome as hers had been.

Even though Gary wanted a family like Carol's, he had no idea of the commitment or skills needed to achieve it. Neither did he realize that, in truth, he really didn't expect very much from marriage. Almost anything would have been better than what he had seen in his parents' marriage. His expectations for marriage, such as they were, had a great deal more to do with what he would get *from* it than what he would give *to* it:

1. He would secure the woman he loved, so that no one else would get her.

2. He would work to pay the bills, while she stayed home to take care of their children.

3. His wife would be a companion who would always be there for him—by his side and on his side.

4. He would get hot meals, a clean house, clean clothes, and a clean bed.

5. He would enjoy sex without guilt.

6. They would be friends—except he would more or less be calling the shots.

7. They would do lots of fun things with friends.

Gary is embarrassed to admit that that was his list of expectations—selfish as it was. He really wanted a mistress, a maid, and a golden retriever—not a wife! He wanted sex, food, friendship, and lodging. He didn't know he could expect much more.

Carol, on the other hand, had seen that marriage could be more. She wanted far more than Gary could ever imagine was possible:

1. Carol wanted love and affection. (That was easy for Gary to give during courtship, but it didn't seem quite so natural during marriage.)

2. She wanted the pleasure of Gary's company. (She assumed he would want to be with her, not work all the time.)

3. She wanted to talk a whole lot. She wanted to tell Gary all about her day and she wanted him to tell her all about his day. (Gary thought adults just came home and watched television.)

4. She wanted a slow, thoughtful approach to the bedroom, so that she could be sure that she was cherished. (Gary just wanted to "get to it.")

5. She wanted Gary to spend time with their children. (Gary wanted to, but wondered when he would find the time. He expected Carol to understand that he "would when he could.")

6. Carol wanted a partnership, where her opinion was valued. (Gary wanted the feeling that he was taking responsibility for his house—all of it.)

As you might imagine, Gary was a first-class disappointment as a husband for the first several years of his marriage. By the grace of God, Carol waited for him to get his act together. She waited patiently while he began to conceive of a marriage that better matched her expectations. He had come to realize that these were the expectations God would bless. Her expectations were the kind and quality that would fill the empty spots and touch their more intimate needs. She waited for him to own those expectations as his own, and begin to grow into them.

Most marriages that fall apart do so under the weight of unfulfilled expectations, both reasonable and unreasonable. It is never too late to discover your mate's expectations. Knowing these expectations will enable you to help your mate fulfill them.

It is good to know what your expectations were and are for marriage. The best way to begin a journey is to find out where you are and determine how to reach your destination. In order to help you do this, we suggest you journal your way through the following questions.

WHAT ARE MY EXPECTATIONS FOR MY MARRIAGE?

Answer these multiple-choice questions. You will be given an opportunity to write your personal thoughts about each of the expectations covered:

1. *When I got married, I hoped my mate and I would want to spend time with each other—both quality and quantity time.*
   a. I believe we have met that hope.
   b. We spend quality but not quantity time.
   c. We spend quantity but not quality time.
   d. We spend neither quality nor quantity time.

Take the time to write down how you feel about the time you spend with your mate. Comment on the factors that are affecting you in a good way and those that are a disappointment to you.

_____

_____

_____

_____

_____

_____

_____

_____

_____

_____

Sample:

We spend quality time together but I wish there were more time. My husband's work includes business trips, more than are comfortable. He is a good provider, and I am proud of his accomplishments. But sometimes I think I would rather endure a little financial hardship to be able to see him more. When we are together we do talk at a satisfying level and he doesn't carry the job home. I have the feeling he would rather be at home more too, and that he thinks this period is just a temporary inconvenience. But I fear it could last longer, and that eventually the absence will create a vacuum that will damage our marriage. I don't know how to express those fears to my husband, when I know he thinks he is doing this for me and our security.

2. When I got married, I had a definite idea about how men and women relate to each other in marriage.
   a. I thought husbands and wives were partners, different but equal.
   b. I thought males were the head of the house and females submitted to them.
   c. I enjoyed being mothered or fathered, and way down deep I just wanted my mate to take care of me.
   d. I thought marriage was just like two friends hanging out in the same place—so that they stay pretty much individuals.
   e. Other _____
      _____

Now, write down your original or current expectations and how your marriage matches up with them.

_____
_____
_____
_____
_____

Now that you get the idea, record your expectations for marriage in other areas. The following is a list of areas on which you can expand.

1. *I believe married couples should handle their finances in the following way.*
   a. Men should do the checkbook.
   b. Women should do the checkbook.
   c. The more financially gifted of the two should do the checkbook.

What financial principles do you believe should govern the management of your money? What percentage of the family's income should go for housing, food, transportation, clothing, insurance, soft goods, entertainment? What should you give to church or other important causes?

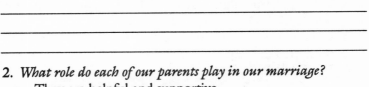

2. *What role do each of our parents play in our marriage?*
   a. They are helpful and supportive.
   b. They are hurtful.
   c. Just how are they affecting our marriage? If we are not married, how do we anticipate that our parents will affect our marriage? If we anticipate problems, what will we do to set boundaries to keep them from hurting our marriage?

About this Sculpture . . .

This fired porcelain sculpture has been handmade and individually hand painted according to the precise instructions of Max Greiner, Jr. The medium of porcelain was invented centuries ago by the Chinese. It is still a beautiful medium for creative expression.

"Divine Servant" ®

Artist, Max Greiner Jr. with the #3 life-size "Divine Servant"® bronze sculpture.

About the Artist . . .

Born in December of 1951, Max Greiner, Jr. has been an artist all his life. Max credits God with any talents he may have. Encouraged by godly parents and teachers, Max graduated from Texas A&M University with a degree in design in 1974. After practicing architecture and then advertising, Max began his career as an independent, professional artist in 1978.

Greiner art work has been created in a variety of forms and styles. Max has refused to specialize in one area like most artists, preferring instead to explore the limits of his imagination. This has resulted in drawings, paintings, sculpture, jewelry, architecture, photography, writing and an assortment of art gift designs.

Today Greiner work can be found in private and corporate collections in all 50 states and more than a dozen countries. Greiner designs have been featured in a number of catalogs including the Wild Wings Original Art Collection, Orvis, David Kay, Abbey Press and the United States Military Mail Order Catalog. Max's art and testimony have been featured nationally and internationally on television, radio, and in magazines and newspapers. The "700 Club" television show aired to households in 50 countries. Over $400,000 has been raised through the sale of Greiner art for wildlife conservation, education, medical and Christian nonprofit causes.

Max is an Eagle Scout. In the past he has served as the Chairman of the American Wildlife Education Foundation, and President of the National Bowhunter Education Foundation. Max and his family live in the beautiful Texas hill country, surrounded by wildlife. They publish an internationally circulated Art Newsletter and catalog. These publications are used as vehicles to share the Good News of Jesus Christ.

About "Divine Servant"®...

*In the Spring of 1986, I believe God clearly directed me to create a sculpture of Jesus washing the feet of His disciple, Peter. God's still, soft voice came to me at the age of 34, during the height of serious personal problems. This was a time when God was teaching me about priorities and humility. He was sculpting me, chipping away the parts that didn't look like Jesus. The first bronze casting of **"Divine Servant"**® was completed in the Spring of 1989.*

"Divine Servant" ® was commissioned by God, not man. It is a message of servanthood, humility and love. I am thankful He chose my hands, and gave me the artistic ability to create this work. I have strived to make this artwork as accurate as possible, and have sought the guidance of the Holy Spirit. My primary scriptural reference for the sculpture came from John 13:1-17. In preparation for the sculpture, I actually experienced the foot washing ceremony with my wife, Sherry, and a Christian friend, to better understand Christ's example. I sculpted Jesus strong and deliberate, power under control. Peter is submitted, but uneasy and confused.

Other references for my art included a book which showed photographs of drawings of Christ and Peter, made by an unknown first century artist. These drawings were found in the catacombs, and are reported to be the oldest known portraits of the men. The sculpture's faces were based on these drawings, and prayer. However, I did use models to study anatomy. The foot washing bowl, which has a footrest, is based on an actual ceramic basin discovered in the Holy Land, which dates back to the time of Jesus. Throughout the entire creation process, I asked God to guide my hands so this artwork would represent a true likeness, and that its existence be a continuous witness to the world.

"Divine Servant"® , I think, has more to do with witnessing and communicating Christ's love, than it does with art. I am amazed at the ways God is using this artwork, from the smallest version to the 1200 pound life-size bronze, to bless His people around the world. It is my prayer that God uses the "Divine Servant"® to expand His kingdom until Jesus returns.

This porcelain is distributed
to fine stores by:

Roman Inc.
555 Lawrence Ave.
Roselle, IL 60172-1599

Yours in Christ,

Max Greiner Jr.

3. *What role will each of us play in the rearing of our children?*
   a. Will Mom stay home and raise our child or children?
   b. Will we both work? If so, who will care for the children?
   c. Will Dad stay home and care for the children?
   d. When home, will one parent relieve the other in the care of the children? (Men:) Do I see child-rearing as women's work, or as something in which I should fully participate?

   _____

   _____

   _____

   _____

4. *How will we use our recreational time?*
   a. We will have time together, and individual time.
   b. We will each choose to do our own thing.
   c. We will do everything together whether we like to or not.

   _____

   _____

   _____

   _____

5. *How will we keep our marriage romantic?*
   a. Romance isn't as important in marriage as it was in courtship.
   b. We will continue dates and romantic getaways even when children come and schedules seem very tight.
   c. We will verbalize our love often.
   d. We will give gifts of love and time to encourage our romance.
   e. Other _____

   _____

   _____

   _____

6. *What is our expectation concerning the role God will play in our marriage?*
   a. Will our marriage be subject to the Bible in all things? If not, which things will go undirected by the Bible?
   b. Will prayer have a place in our home? When?
   c. As a married couple, do we intend to give financially to our church or to parachurch organizations? How much?
   d. Because our promises concerning marriage were made to God and to each other, will we ask God for the strength to keep them?
   e. Will we worship together regularly?
   f. Will we seek friends who love God and share our faith in him?

_____

_____

_____

7. *Where will our career(s) fit into our marriage? How will we guard our marriage so that our career(s) does not interfere with it?*

_____

_____

_____

8. *What are our sexual expectations for marriage?*
   a. What things do we think are appropriate for married couples to do together?
   b. Are there sexual activities that make us feel uncomfortable enough to prefer not to participate in them?
   c. How often would we like to be sexual together?
   d. Can we each explain to our partner what makes us feel loved and physically satisfied?

_____

_____

_____

Remember, no one can fill another's expectations in every area. Marital bliss is a lot like a batting average in baseball. The greatest hitter of all time was Rogers Hornsby, who batted .426—just less than one out of two times he came to bat. If your mate is meeting half of your needs, you probably have a pretty good marriage. If he or she is not doing that well right now, you can still hope for growth. While you are waiting, you can develop friendships with members of your own sex that can help fill in the gaps. Some of those gaps your mate will never fill, and some he or she will. You can be proactive in helping your own situation. The most important thing is that you make clear to your mate your hopes and dreams for your marriage.

It would not be wise to tell your mate *all* of your unfulfilled hopes as you begin this journey. Give him or her time to think through these kinds of exercises before you have an in-depth discussion.

If your mate is not likely to read this kind of material, don't give up hope. Begin by discussing your partner's hopes and dreams for marriage. Ask, "What did your parents do that helped or hurt you?" Move through the areas one by one until you know each other's dreams.

One final note concerning expectations: If your expectations are reasonable, you will be putting your effort into something that can be for you a garden of delights.

If your expectations are too high, you will be disappointed, frustrated, and disillusioned with your marriage.

As we journey together through this book, be ready to raise or lower your expectations. With up-to-the-minute adjustments, you may design a much more fulfilling plan than you ever dreamed of.

TWO

༄

He Made Them Male and Female

O n the fifth and sixth days of Creation, God made 4,400,000 different kinds of animals. The vast majority he made male and female. Interestingly, a select few, hermaphrodites, are both male and female. In mating they can both fertilize and be fertilized. However, God made most species male and female, assigning to each a very specific way of behaving toward and responding to the opposite sex.

During Gary's seven years working at the Los Angeles Zoo, nothing intrigued him more than observing animals relating as male and female in courtship rituals and the rearing of young. Let's look at several examples, noting how the behavior of animals is strikingly similar to that of humans.

When the female black widow spider is in heat, the male approaches her web with great care. He is terribly aroused, but proceeds carefully. Instinctively, he knows he is in great danger. She is four times larger than he is. Besides that, she is blind. One false step and he would be mistaken for just another unsuspecting insect that might stumble into her web. So he takes the essential time to court her. He does so by gently plucking her web in just the right time signature. Relaxing in her web, she responds to this one-note love song. He then dashes a few steps onto the web while she is in her swoon. Then he plucks again. Even his few steps awaken within her deadly beauty a latent predatory urge to kill. Again she swoons, and again he dashes forward, repeating the process until he is by her side. He gently reaches out and strokes her abdomen, now bulging with eggs. She waits to be fertilized. When he senses her willingness to mate, they join together. This one mating encounter will provide enough sperm to create at least one silky white egg sack, producing up to 125 young.

When the process is finished, the male spider is exhausted and she is aroused. Attempting to crawl from the web, he often stumbles. In a blink of an eye she is on him, sinking her deadly mandibles into his frail white body. He becomes food for her and her developing young. In nature, nothing is wasted. The event of his death isn't personal—it's just that the female is compelled by instinct to enjoy touch for the bearing of young. She is not looking for an abiding relationship because spiders are not concerned with intimacy. Even when the young are born, she merely lets them crawl away, caring not if they live or die.

Elephants are matriarchal like the black widow, but they do not kill their mates. For a two-week period each year, the herds of female elephants and their young permit the approach of the adult males. The males are compelled by odors in the wind to join the females for mating. Any other time of year, the males would be savagely driven away from the female herds. But for two blissful weeks the males are welcomed. When the male elephant is still young yet mature enough to survive, he is driven from the herd to find other males. The young females, on the other hand, remain with their mothers for several years.

Sea lions live in a harem system. The very large males find their way to beaches and rocky areas and establish a territory in what is called a rookery. The stronger and more aggressive the male, the larger the territory he is able to claim. By the time the females arrive, the territories are established and the males set about claiming females for their harems. The females are already pregnant and soon begin to give birth to fragile and helpless pups. As they did the year before, the males again impregnate their harem even as they are caring for their newborn pups. The males are never free from the task of maintaining their territories, and can be seen all day long hurling themselves from one end of their territories to the other, defending their boundaries. They are not at all careful. In the process of defending their territories, females are injured and pups are crushed to death. The males stand proud and arrogant, ruling their little kingdoms at all too high a price to their families.

Rattlesnakes meet by chance and breed with little formality. A brief time later, the female gives birth to live young. Then, each of the young crawl in a different direction, as did their parents before them.

Canadian geese mate for life, as do all geese and swans. They are so bonded to each other that, if one is injured, the other will not go on without it. It stays beside its injured mate to provide comfort and defense. If the mate dies, it is not uncommon to see the other mourn so deeply that it loses the will to live and die of starvation.

Gray wolves also mate for life. They live in small family units most of the year with a male, a female, and an uncle or aunt. Most of their daily diet is field mice; they only form packs to hunt larger animals such as elk, moose, and caribou while the rodents are hibernating for the winter. Male and female wolves both care equally for the young. Wolves are devoted, sacrificial parents and devoted, sacrificial mates. They are bonded and faithful. (Isn't it odd that promiscuous human males are referred to as wolves?)

The male pied hornbill, a large Asian bird, finds a hole in a tree into which he drives the female. After breeding, he seals her in the nest with mud, filling all but a peephole. She lays eggs and incubates them. Everything she eats or drinks is pushed through that little opening by the male, until the day that the young are ready to leave the nest. On that day, the male chips away the mud and frees his family. He is the epitome of the controlling mate.

God designed a relationship for each male and female he created. Each behavior is specific and unique to its species. The roles are clear-cut. When we view humanity, however, the roles of the male and female become confused. Men and women do not exhibit the consistent behavior displayed by other animals. Some men and women remind us of the behavior seen in black widow spiders. They leave devastated, emasculated mates in their wake. Then they abandon their young. Some human males, like sea lions, are far more concerned with career and possessions than with family. Abused wives, and children with wounded spirits, are their legacy. Like rattlers, some humans mate and crawl away, and no one cares for their young. Then again, we see deeply devoted and bonded couples, serving each other and their children as do geese and wolves. And finally we see mates who like Asian hornbills exhibit unreasonable and unyielding control, smothering each other with demands and declarations.

As we look at human behavior, we must come to one of two conclusions: As a species, either we have not been assigned a way to relate as male and female, or there is a prescribed way of relating but we've chosen to ignore it. It is not logical that God would have assigned 4,400,000 animals a way to relate, male and female, and overlooked mankind. It is clear that the latter conclusion is the valid one: We have been assigned a method and we are not following it.

The clearest articulation of our male and female roles and behaviors is found beginning with Ephesians 5:21, which describes what God intended Christian marriage to be:

Be subject to one another out of reverence for Christ.

Ephesians 5:21 (RSV)

The word *subject*, or *submit*, does not translate into *obey*. And the word *obey* is not found in Scripture in reference to wives, but in reference to slaves and children. *Subject* is a grander word, meaning *to yield willingly or relinquish your rights, not because you have to, but because you want to, in the best interest of the common good.* It represents the same dynamic as would be found if a king or queen of a foreign country moved to America, relinquishing his or her royal authority in order to become a citizen here. In order to settle in America, the king or queen would have to give up exclusive power and become subject to our constitution. He or she would have to give up the idea of directing the lives of others, learning instead to accommodate and fit in.

In a Christian marriage we are to be subject one to another. We learn how to fit in, or better said, *fit together.* The passage declares that a husband ought to revere his wife as his own queen, and a wife ought to revere her husband as her own king: *Each of us are commanded to give up our own rights to serve our mates.* We become subjects of the king or the queen. We come to marriage as male and female, with all the uniqueness that accompanies gender. However, in the sense of dual subjection, we enter marriage as equals: Equal both in servanthood and in royalty.

MARRIAGE: A ROYAL ARRANGEMENT

To develop this theme of dual-royalty and dual-subjection in marriage, let's look at some of the behaviors that a husband *(king)* would want to experience from his wife *(subject)*, and that a wife *(queen)* would hope to experience from her husband *(subject)*.

The husband, a noble and virtuous king, would want:
- to be respected
- to be loved and valued
- to be encouraged
- to be touched and held
- to know that his counsel is valued
- to enjoy praise for his victories

- his partner's faithfulness and loyalty
- his subjects to feel safe in his care
- a close friend and confidante

He wouldn't want:
- to be taken for granted
- to be feared
- to feel alone
- to be patronized
- subjects who bring him shame
- a dirty castle (and he shouldn't mess it up himself!)

The wife, a noble and virtuous queen, would want:
- to be highly valued
- to be respected
- to be loved and cherished
- to be listened to and talked to
- to feel safe and secure
- to be free to achieve her goals and dreams
- to be admired for her person and her gifts
- to be touched and held
- to be remembered well and spoken of highly
- to have pure, undefiled love
- to voice her wishes in the moments of decision that affect her life and the lives of her children
- her words to be treasured and kept in the vault of confidence
- playful surprises

She wouldn't want:
- to be minimized
- to be intimidated
- to be taken for granted
- to be a low priority

The relationship of a husband and wife is a divinely designed partnership, each acting in the best interest of the other for the common good. Each exercises strengths and accommodates each other's needs and wants. Unlike animals, who obey their instincts because they *have to* obey them, we choose to obey God's design for marriage because we *want* to. We trust that God knows best how to direct us through the relationship he himself designed.

ALIGNED WITH GOD'S DESIGN

We choose individually how we live out our role in the marriage. There is a chance that you will fulfill your role as God instructed, and that your mate will not. Sensitive to that possibility, God has built in a measure of comfort for us. He said to "be subject one to another out of reverence to Christ": Even if your mate doesn't respond to or appreciate your efforts to be a good partner, you can be sure that Christ will value your efforts. He will receive your obedience to subjection as a reverence to him. Life is more about pleasing God than about pleasing your mate.

If only it were possible to guarantee contentment in marriage! Unfortunately, it is not. The one area over which we have a measure of control is our own contribution to the marriage relationship. We can't know for sure how that contribution will be received, except by Christ. But even in a fallen world, playing out the role God has designed for us will give us the very best shot at happiness.

After establishing the foundational principle of *mutual subjection* or *partnership*, the apostle Paul in Ephesians goes on to describe in more detail what is expected individually of a wife and a husband. It seems that husbands often know what is expected of wives, and wives know what is expected of husbands, but neither can quote what God expects of them. We like to read each other's mail! We want to hold others more responsible or accountable to their tasks than we would hold ourselves. This is not one of our species' more noble characteristics!

In the best interest of your marriage, we ask you to spend most of your time thinking about what God is saying to *you* in the passages that address you as husband or wife. Forget for a moment your mate's assignment, and focus your attention on your own role.

If your mate does not know his or her assigned role, pray that he or she will seek out that information. It is not your responsibility to inform your mate. Somehow, referring our mates to things they "should know about" always comes across as criticism. Putting ourselves in the place of our mate helps us see what tender territory this is. If you were given a book by your mate with exact instructions for becoming an excellent marriage partner, wouldn't you assume that you were being corrected for some shortcoming? Learning about our own role and pouring ourselves into that role is a full-time effort. The only real changes any of us can make are our own personal changes. It is good to know that doing so makes the greatest impact in our lives and brings the greatest fulfillment!

WORDS TO WIVES

In Ephesians 5:22-24 (RSV), Paul goes on to say,

> Wives be subject to your husbands as to the Lord. For the husband is the head of the wife as Christ is the head of the church, his body, and is himself its Savior. As the church is subject to Christ, so let wives also be subject in everything to their husbands.

This verse offers fifty-two concise words of direction to wives. First, let's consider what the words *do not mean*. These words do not mean that the wife must obey her husband's every request. Rather, she must comply with requests her husband makes that are in line with the will of God. The husband is free to ask his wife *only* those things which are aligned with God's will. When a husband conducts himself within the context of God's will, loving his wife as Christ loves the church (which is a tall order!), a wife will yield to the will of God as requested by her husband. Christ's love for the church is characterized by sacrifice, not by a demanding attitude. Christ's love for the church led him to "give his very life to take care of it and to be its Savior" (Ephesians 5:23, LB). The proper response to such love is expressed clearly in verse 24: "As the church is subject to Christ, so let wives also be subject in everything to their husbands" (RSV).

God would never permit a husband to ask his wife to lie for him, steal for him, or violate her conscience for him. The wife must never be asked to endure any form of abuse from her husband. Scripture does not teach that a wife should comply with a husband's inappropriate demands. (In future chapters, we will be elaborating on the topic of responding to inappropriate demands.) God gives husbands a tremendous responsibility to live within his design and make certain that their requests to their wives are part of that design. God's design is that the husband, rather than having a demanding attitude, would always want to operate in the best interest of his wife. The wife, likewise, conducts herself in the best interest of her husband. Both submit to the other.

The point bears repeating: The Bible never says that a wife must yield to *any* demand of her husband, but only to those aligned with God's will. We hope that a review of these Scriptures, read in context, will clarify your role as a wife and free you from misunderstandings you may have regarding the interactive roles of husband and wife.

FOR HUSBANDS ONLY

While Paul gave women 52 words of direction in Ephesians 5, his instructions for men total 164 words—indicating perhaps the level of responsibility given to the man in marriage. Or perhaps it is because women, by nature, are more adept at relationships than men, requiring less direction. Here are Paul's words for men:

> Husbands, love your wives, as Christ loved the church and gave himself up for her, that he might sanctify her, having cleansed her by the washing of water with the word, that he might present the church to himself in splendor, without spot or wrinkle or any such thing, that she might be holy and without blemish. Even so husbands should love their wives as their own bodies. He who loves his wife loves himself. For no man ever hates his own flesh, but nourishes and cherishes it as Christ does the church, because we are members of his body. "For this reason a man shall leave his father and mother and be joined to his wife, and the two shall become one flesh."
>
> This mystery is a profound one, and I am saying that it refers to Christ and the church; however, let each one of you love his wife as himself, and let the wife see that she respects her husband.   **Ephesians 5:25-33 (RSV)**

What, specifically, does Paul ask of men?

1. The husband is to be subject to his wife, as she is to him (v. 21).

2. The husband is to love the wife in a wholehearted and sacrificial way. The zinger is that men are asked to love their wives as Christ loved the church. That means sacrificially, an all-out, total commitment, bar nothing. There is a definite *she-first*, not *me-first* attitude here (v. 25).

3. The husband must set his wife apart in such a way that his love brings out the very best in her. He is to help her be everything she is capable of being, everything God intended for her to be (v. 26).

4. The husband is to love his wife as he loves himself. This involves both nurturing and cherishing (v. 28).

5. The husband is to position the wife at the very top of his relational priorities, even above his father and mother. Only God is to be more revered than the wife—not children, nor friends, nor anyone or anything else (v. 31).

Clearly, the husband is *not* to be the chairman of the board, the quarterback, the foreman, or the boss, much less the sole and reigning tyrannical monarch. Understood in context, Ephesians 5 condemns a *"me man, you woman"* attitude. What is described in these passages is a loving, caring, nurturing, responsible, devoted, sacrificing partner. The Ephesians 5 husband is a partner who will sacrifice his wishes, even himself, in an effort to promote the flourishing of his lifetime partner.

THE MARRIAGE PARTNERSHIP

Human nature makes it difficult to join into a productive partnership, whether we are male or female. We fight for an edge, and seek a *one-up* position. Both men and women are capable of turning a marriage into a cold war, a hot war, a competition, a convenience arrangement, a fling, a prison sentence, or a contest of wills. That was not what God intended for us. Marriage was designed to be a partnership.

What does this partnership look like?

1. The marriage partnership is a contractual agreement, entered into voluntarily by a man and a woman. The man and the woman make promises before God and witnesses that indicate they will love and care for each other until they are separated by death. They sign papers which bind together their assets and any future produce of the marriage, including financial gain and children born of or adopted into the marriage. Unless otherwise arranged, the partners begin the marriage in a fifty-fifty contract, in which property is owned jointly and managed together. Each voluntarily relinquishes exclusive power and rights.

2. As with any good partnership, trust is foundational to marriage. No other foundation is sufficient to support the weight of the institution. Trust develops over a long period of time. Commitment, integrity, and faithfulness will contribute to the growth of trust in the partnership.

3. In a good partnership there will be equal sharing of profit and loss. The good times and the bad times will be shared by both of the partners.

4. In a good partnership there is a fair distribution of responsibility. Roles will be defined, agreed upon, and adjusted as needed.

5. In a good partnership both partners enjoy veto power. Each marriage partner must have a say in the life of the marriage and the family.

6. In a good partnership personal giftedness must be considered when assigning responsibility. We are living in an age that recognizes more than ever before the value of both male and female. Who handles the finances, who handles the cooking or shopping or child care, or the decorating

and upkeep of the home, should be based on giftedness, not on any preconceived notion about male or female roles. In Galatians 3:28 we discover that in Christ there is no distinction, no "male nor female."

7. In a good partnership the emphasis is on fixing problems—not on fixing blame.

8. In a good partnership there is open communication and full disclosure of information.

9. In a good partnership there is an effective system for the resolution of conflicts.

10. In a good partnership one partner promotes the success of the other partner.

11. In a good partnership each partner is willing to take responsibility for his failures and mistakes, and each promotes recovery in the other.

12. In a good partnership each partner makes it a high priority to invest in the maintenance of the partnership.

In addition to these general principles of partnership, the partnership of marriage includes some unique qualities, exclusive to marriage. First, it is a sacred relationship based on promises made to and before God. Second, it is sealed by God, with only a very few specified reasons as conditions for dissolution. The partnership of marriage is by nature a romantic and sexual relationship, creating an intimate bond which exceeds any platonic relationship. This bond is designed to endure throughout one or both of the partners' lives. Marriage is a unique partnership: it depends on love in order to succeed.

In *The Message*, his paraphrase of the New Testament,

Eugene Peterson renders 1 Peter 3:4-7 in a way that presents marriage as a loving partnership.

> Cultivate inner beauty, the gentle gracious kind that God delights in. The holy women of old were beautiful before God that way, and were good, loyal wives to their husbands. Sarah for instance, taking care of Abraham, would address him as, "My dear husband." You'll be true daughters of Sarah if you do the same, unanxious and unintimidated.
>
> The same goes for you husbands: Be good husbands to your wives. Honor them, delight in them. As women they lack some of your advantages. But, in the new life of God's grace you are equals. Treat your wives, then, as equals so your prayers don't run aground.

IS MY MARRIAGE A LOVING PARTNERSHIP?

Answer the following discussion questions to evaluate your marriage:

1. Discuss how you plan to maintain the marriage partnership in terms of combining your assets, and loving and caring for each other "till death do us part."

2. Discuss the importance of trust to the marriage relationship. How do you plan to be trustworthy in both the small things and the monumental things?

3. Consider ways you can encourage your mate in the event of loss or disappointment. What people have been an encouragement to each of you, and how can you emulate their examples?

4. How do each of you define your everyday roles? Are you comfortable with what you have agreed upon or are currently practicing? If you know of changes which would be an improvement in some way, make suggestions to each other and evaluate the ideas together.

5 Do you believe that as a couple you practice open communication, where each of you speaks your opinions, preferences and feelings?

6. When there is conflict, do you look for solutions together or find yourselves arguing? (See chapter ten, "Arguing for Fun and Profit.")

7. Discuss how you look for opportunities to support each other's growth and success. Offer specific examples.

8. Discuss the importance of taking responsibility for one's own actions, including mistakes. In addition, discuss ways you can promote each other's recovery from failures or mistakes by encouraging and showing understanding while the partner makes corrections.

THREE

∾

A Person of Substance: Commitment and Integrity

Dane and Patsy drove away from the church amid hoots and hoorays on the way to what Patsy had been told would be a Fantasy Island Honeymoon. They were running a little late and Patsy could feel Dane tightening up as they hit stop-and-go traffic five miles from Stapleton Airport in Denver. He cursed under his breath that he hoped that there was some blood to show for the inconvenience he was experiencing.

Patsy said, "Dane! You shouldn't talk like that. We have plenty of time."

Dane gave Patsy a sarcastic smirk but remained sullenly silent as he stared at the car in front of them. "Let's go!" he exploded.

Patsy had not seen Dane this moody before. She tried to rub his neck to relax him but he shoved her hand away, continuing to just stare ahead. Patsy stayed quiet for a while, but it was her nature to try to make things better. Breaking the silence, she said, "Tell me about our Fantasy Island Honeymoon, Dane."

Dane barked back at her, "Give me a break, Patsy! Trust me! It's a surprise and it's going to stay a surprise for a while longer. If we ever get to the airport, you'll find out anyway! Much more of this and I'll wish we'd stayed home."

They arrived at the airport in plenty of time but the traffic had put Dane in a *mood*. He was snappy with baggage handlers and reservations clerks, and tipped no one.

As they settled into their seats, Dane focused on the shortcomings of Pan Am Airlines: The seats were too close together; the bags of peanuts were too small; the in-flight movie was stupid; and the cabin temperature was too hot.

By now Patsy knew that they were going to a private resort in the Bahamas, but Dane was so busy complaining and whining that she was unable to get any further details so that she could imagine how wonderful their honeymoon was going to be. It certainly wasn't much yet! But Patsy, being a positive romantic, thought everything would get better once they got there.

Then, Patsy began to feel weak and clammy and nauseated. Although the flight was smooth, she wrote it off to air sickness. Then her joints began to ache. Then, as if that were not bad enough, she got the worst headache she had ever had. When they landed in the Bahamas, she asked Dane if they could go to the local hospital before they went to the resort. He called the resort and discovered there was a doctor who could see Patsy in his office near the resort when they arrived.

The visit to the doctor's office was the first kind treatment Patsy had experienced since the wedding kiss several hours before. The doctor told her that she had a nasty flu. Patsy had a temperature of 103° and felt terrible. The resort shuttled Patsy and Dane to their room, and Patsy immediately went to bed.

Patsy asked Dane if he would mind getting a bottle of Seven-Up and some ice and soda crackers. On his way to the pop machine Dane saw several couples playing tennis and they invited him to join them. He thought, "Maybe later," and completed his errand for Patsy.

When Dane returned to the room he found Patsy in the bathroom relinquishing everything she had eaten on the plane. He helped her back to bed and asked, "You through doing that for a while?"

Patsy said she thought she was.

"I'll tell you what, Patsy. No use both of us wasting away in our room. Some couples asked me if I wanted to join them playing a little tennis. I'll come back and check on you now and then and make sure you're okay. I'd kiss ya, but I don't want to get the crud—if you know what I mean!" Patsy was deeply hurt that Dane would leave her alone, but tried to understand it from his point of view.

Dane was gone for four hours. When he returned, Patsy was deluged with all of his tennis exploits—four hours' worth!

Later that evening Dane asked, "Patsy, when would you like to fool around a little?"

Exasperated that he would even ask, she told Dane, "I can't believe you're even asking!" Dane jumped on her for displaying an "attitude."

Patsy wondered if she had made a big mistake, the biggest of her life. She had never felt so lonely. The next three days of the honeymoon were just like the first. She was left alone in the room to recuperate while Dane "partied on." Their last three days were colored by the first four. Patsy was quiet, hurt, and withdrawn.

When they returned home, Dane made matters worse by recounting to all the relatives and friends how Patsy "waited till the honeymoon to get the flu! But no problem! I made the best of it anyway!"

The honeymoon was over! And that's no overstatement! Dane threw himself into his job at an advertising firm. During the courtship he had cut back his hours to secure Patsy as his wife; now he resumed his former pattern. "Now is the time to make up for lost time," was the way Dane put it. Seventy-hour work weeks became the norm and Patsy felt very abandoned.

When she called attention to Dane's schedule and how she never saw him anymore, Dane exploded. He told her he was doing it for her, and berated her for her lack of appreciation. He protested, "I can't handle the thought of being poor! Someday you will be glad I wanted to make something of myself!"

Patsy grew increasingly lonely. Rather than staying at home alone all the time, she decided to call some old girlfriends and do something with them. She slowly filled up the time she had reserved for Dane with her friends. It wasn't what she wanted, but it would have to do until Dane decided to "play marriage" again.

Dane ate, drank, and slept advertising, and found himself lonely in the midst of it all. He found himself asking women associates if they were busy for lunch. That's when he met Beth. Beth was attractive, fun-loving, married, and *lonely*. Her husband was like Dane: very ambitious and away on business trips most of the time. She found herself very attracted to Dane. After three weeks of business lunches, she offered to make Dane lunch at her condo. She explained that her husband was away and she wanted Dane to see her artwork, a sideline she was very good at.

The affair had begun. It continued for months. Patsy sensed something was wrong, but she was a very trusting person. As Dane showed a steady decline in sexual interest and even increased his long hours, Patsy became more and more unhappy. She shared her situation with her best girlfriend, Sheila. Sheila's first response was, "Patsy, I hope you know Dane's cheating on you."

Patsy resisted believing. But as time passed, she knew something was wrong. At Sheila's constant goading Patsy decided to hire a private detective. She had pictures and phone recordings in her hands within three days. Over Dane's protests, Patsy filed for divorce. Their marriage ended one month short of their first anniversary.

* * *

Unfortunately, this sad story is true and reflects a predator that we see all too often in marriages: a lack of commitment and integrity.

Dane displayed a lack of commitment to Patsy in a number of ways:

1. He had promised to love and cherish Patsy, as Christ loved and cherished the church. Instead, he gave her sarcasm, anger, and silence.

2. He had hidden his moodiness from Patsy during their courtship. Now, his lack of regard for Patsy was on display in living technicolor as he lashed out at her with his short temper.

3. His desire for physical recreation took priority over his responsibility to care for the needs of his wife in her illness.

4. He demonstrated a lack of commitment by seeking to satisfy his sexual needs without regard for his wife's health.

5. He missed an opportunity to show his commitment to Patsy by staying close to her while she was feeling ill. He could have brought comfort through keeping her company, rubbing her aching body, offering her sips of water, and assuring her of his concern.

TILL DEATH DO US PART

Marriages are built on the cornerstones of *love*, *honesty*, *integrity*, and *commitment*. When in place and in abundance, these cornerstones create a fortress around a marriage—keeping it safe from predators.

These four cornerstones are interlinked. Love has no substance without honesty, integrity, and commitment. Feelings can and often do change during the course of a marriage. When feelings fluctuate, integrity and commitment stand guard duty over the life of a marriage.

As valuable as honesty is, when truth is spoken without love it cuts into your relationship like a sword. Integrity and commitment stand guard against this cruel and damaging kind of truth.

What good would integrity and commitment be if there was no love and no honesty? There would be nothing worth cherishing. Love, honesty, integrity, and commitment are essential and must be present at the same time for a relationship to be healthy and strong.

While the four cornerstones work together, we would like to expand on the roles of *integrity* and *commitment*. We see these character traits as essential to building a *till death us do part* kind of marriage.

Integrity is a powerful word. Funk and Wagnall's defines it as:

1. Uprightness of character, honesty.
2. The condition or quality of being unimpaired or sound.
3. The state of being complete or undivided.

People of integrity always seek to do the best thing in the marriage. They tell the truth. They are not unpredictable. With them, *what you see is what you get.* They are strong yet transparent, without a hidden evil side. They are not one way one minute and another the next. They keep their word from the beginning.

It is good to remind ourselves of what we as husbands and wives promised from the beginning. Then we should ask the difficult but appropriate question: Are we doing what we said we would do? Have we maintained our commitments? A good definition of commitment is *a long obedience in the same direction* (the title of a book by Eugene Peterson which is one of our favorites).

Vows are central to any marriage ceremony. Whether or not we keep our vows determines whether or not any of us can lay any claim to being persons of integrity or persons of commitment. Marriage vows usually include several kinds of commitments or promises. Read the following vow. Have you made or do you plan to make these promises in your wedding vows?

I, _____, take thee, _____, as God's gift to be my wife/husband.

I do promise and covenant, before God and these witnesses,
To be thy loving and faithful husband/wife.
In sickness and in health,
In joy and in sorrow,
In plenty and want,
For as long as we both shall live.
I will cherish you above all others
And to you only will I pledge my faithfulness.

These vows reflect that:

- We have made a sacred promise before God and witnesses.

- We promised to be loving (considerate, kind, gentle, affectionate, adoring, sacrificial, passionate, thoughtful).

- We promised to be sexually intimate with our mate *only*.

- We promised to be loving and faithful whether our mate is healthy or in poor health.

- We promised to be loving and faithful whether rich or poor.

- We promised to be loving and faithful during good times and bad times.

- We promised to be loving and faithful until we are parted by death.

- We promised to be loving and faithful and to cherish (highly value and esteem) each other above all others.

Will our vows be tested in marriage? Of course they will be. Why else would we need to make them? The vows stand as a fortress, a wall that prevents us from walking away from our marriage. It is when we hit the wall that we are compelled by our integrity and commitment to keep our vows.

C.S. Lewis wrote an article for the *Saturday Evening Post* titled "No Right to Happiness," in which he addresses one of the greatest lies of our day—the idea that happiness is our main purpose in life. Lewis said we have no right to personal happiness if we are obtaining it by overruling the will of God. We must find our happiness within the will of God. We cannot sacrifice the will of God on the altar of our own perceived need to be happy. Our purpose is and remains that we love God and serve him all the days of our life.

IN SICKNESS AND IN HEALTH

When we make our marriage vows, most of us haven't taken the time to think about what would happen if one of the partners became incapacitated or chronically ill or even mentally ill. By nature we are optimistic about our future as a couple, and we don't anticipate tragedy; yet tragedies happen, and when they do they can devastate a marriage. Following are some situations that people we know have had to face. What would you do if you were faced with a similar situation? What would your spouse do? How would your marriage vows apply?

A tragic car accident. There was no time to react. Rod looked through the passenger window and saw a large GMC half-ton pickup truck bearing down on his family's Ford Pinto station wagon. A split second later, the truck smashed into the side of the Pinto. Every window was shattered into thousands of pieces. The deafening sound of crashing steel and breaking glass could be heard for blocks. The gas tank ruptured and fumes permeated the inside of the vehicle. The car was hit with such force that it was knocked seventy-five yards down the street, stopping only when it hit an abutment.

Rod yelled frantically to his wife, Carmen, "Get out of the car! There's gas and it could explode!" He then climbed over the front seat to the back, where both daughters, ages six and three, were crying hysterically. The oldest, Jody, was holding her left arm. She was in extreme pain. Rod handed their youngest, Jennifer, out the broken rear window, then began sliding Jody toward the only door of the car that would still open.

Jody looked up at her father and said, "Daddy, you're bleeding!"

Shards of glass had punctured his forehead, and his face was covered with blood. In his concern for his family, he felt nothing but deep fear for his wife and girls. His last concern was himself. He carried Jody twenty-five yards away from the car and bundled her in his coat for warmth. Within minutes, his family was surrounded by people anxious to help and determine the extent of the injuries.

All four of them had survived the accident, although Rod had major concerns about Jody's left arm. As the initial shock passed, Rod became aware of excruciating pain in his hip and lower back. He was sitting next to Jody when the paramedics arrived. When they lifted her into the back of the ambulance, Rod realized he could no longer stand.

In the emergency room, it soon became evident that Rod would never be able to walk normally again. He would have to give up his career as a landscape architect. Rod and Carmen were thankful for their disability insurance, but it only accounted for half of his regular salary. If they were to survive financially and keep their current residence, Carmen would have to find full-time employment.

This would be a major and unwelcome adjustment. Carmen volunteered at Jody's elementary school and was part of a neighborhood babysitting co-op. She would have to leave both of those involvements behind and, with them, give up many happy hours with her children. Rod's life would change drastically, too. He would no longer be able to do the job he loved. Nor would time and love bring about a change. His injury was irreversible.

What were Rod and Carmen to do? They had promised to

be there *for better or for worse,* but had only made plans to accommodate *for better.* Suddenly they had to completely reorder their plans. Nothing, it seemed, would be like they had dreamed. Nothing. They felt hopeless and afraid. Both realized that the only way around this situation was *through* it. They had to make the best out of a bad thing.

Rod's muscular, tanned body began to atrophy and pale, but he mastered the use of the wheelchair rather quickly. Though his legs were an encumbrance, he was able to increase the use and strength of his arms to compensate. While Carmen was away at work in the daytime, he took over management of the household. Rod appreciated Carmen's wholehearted willingness to do her part, but he fought hard for the dignity of knowing that he was doing his part as well. He set out to gain significance from his new role. In no time, Rod had become a decent cook, not only learning everything that Carmen knew, but adding his own imagination to some new culinary delights.

These positive adjustments were often interrupted by days—even weeks—of depression. The hardest pill for Rod to swallow was losing his sense of manhood. His body had changed dramatically. As satisfying as it was to make a good meal, it didn't compare to standing back and gazing at a third-of-an-acre parcel he had transformed into an explosion of color and form. "That sure beat the heck out of finishing the dishes and struggling to master using a vacuum cleaner from the confines of a wheelchair!" he once observed.

One evening, Carmen and Rod lay side by side in bed. She noticed a tear falling from his cheek onto his pillow. Holding him close, she asked him what was wrong. He said with hopelessness in his voice, "I hate the thought that I am half a man to you…. I know we're great friends, but I loved my role when we were both friends and lovers. I'm not that man anymore. I don't know what's worse… the thought that I will never know that kind of pleasure again or that I can never bring that kind of pleasure to you. Both thoughts are horrible to me. Sometimes, I think you would be better off without me."

Both sobbing now, Carmen held him tighter. She spoke softly, "Rod, I married you because you were a great man, not because you were a great lover—though you were. I married you because you had a great heart. I loved you because you were the kind of man everyone admires. You were kind and good, and you always did what you said you would do. I knew when you promised me that you would love me *for better or for worse,* you would have always been there for me no matter what happened. I still have the main things I married you for. I still have you. I still have your heart. And I'm so thankful for what we have, that I don't give much thought to what we *don't* have. Rod, I'm sure we will always miss those things that were taken away by the accident."

Looking into his eyes, she added, "We still have the best part. We have each other. And we always will."

As he listened to the soft, comforting words of his beautiful wife, Rod knew that Carmen loved him not for what he could do for her, not for what he could accomplish with his able body—but just for him, just the way he was. He knew they would adjust to the changes, and they would work together on good days, on days clouded with depression and grief, on all days. He embraced her and said, "I will always love you, Carmen. I know we can do whatever we must together."

* * *

Carmen recognized that she loved Rod for who he was, not for what he did. Her words to Rod reflected her commitment to her wedding vows: "In sickness and in health, for better or for worse...." As a couple, Rod and Carmen talked about their feelings and their role reversals. Rod chose to contribute to the family as best he could by cooking and cleaning while Carmen was at work. It wasn't easy, but they made the necessary adjustments and discovered their love for each other and commitment to working things out.

Most couples speak their vows with sincerity, yet with hopes that the illnesses will be infrequent and short-lived. Most never anticipate that tragedy or sickness might befall them. For that reason we encourage you to discuss the following questions with your spouse.

1. If one of you were suddenly incapacitated and confined to a wheelchair, how would your roles change? How might you make adjustments for such a change? It might be wise to come up with a plan; the old saying "Forewarned is forearmed" applies here.

2. Do your present circumstances assure you of an adequate support system? Are you isolated from extended family and close friends? What steps can you take to cultivate a support system? (For example, become actively involved members of a local church, small group, or Sunday school class and cultivate deeper relationships with family and friends.)

3. Do you have disability insurance? If not, consider getting some. If so, will it be adequate? How can you compensate for the loss of income?

4. A tragedy like Rod and Carmen's can lead to a lower standard of living. Discuss what you would do if you were faced with living on approximately half your current income. How would your plan reflect your commitment to making your marriage a priority? How could you ensure quality of life despite decreased finances? (A sudden decrease in living standard could also result from the loss of a job.)

5. Has your desire for immediate gratification prevented you from preparing a nest egg for unexpected hard times? Savings would not be the whole answer, but would give you a cushion so that the transition to a lower standard of living would be a bearable process, not a traumatic event.

6. Do you value each other more for who you are than for what you do? When people become disabled, their identity

and satisfaction must come from who they are, not from what they can accomplish. What do each of you bring to your relationship because of your character and personalities?

She's no longer the person I used to know. James stared across the courtroom at Joan, remembering better days. When he had married her, she had just graduated from Mountain View High School in Vermont. She was a straight-*A* student, one of the most intelligent women he had ever met. She had a nearly photographic memory, and was both witty and playful. Surrounded by girlfriends, Joan was the envy of her high school... and James was the envy of all the men on campus.

Mutually determining that James needed to finish his education first, Joan took a full-time position in a bank. Not long after, she was promoted to executive secretary. Her boss often told her that she was the only thing in his life that was truly indispensable. She was one of those fortunate people who could be taught something once and have it mastered.

When James completed his college education, Joan decided she would rather start a family than pursue further education. She liked motherhood so much that they decided to have five children—all born at sixteen-month intervals! By this time James had begun his own company; he was the president and founder of Wilson's Business Machines. They owned a beautiful home on sprawling acreage in upstate Vermont. They had become proud participants in the American Dream.

Then the tide began to change. The changes were at first subtle and James wrote them off as eccentricities. He noticed Joan telling the children things most people would consider absurd. She became obsessed with the cleanliness of the school rest rooms, and forbade the children from using them. She told them, "You will become diseased and die if you use them!" James was embarrassed to discover that Joan had actually made an appointment with the school's principal to berate him for the "loathsome condition of the rest rooms!"

The next oddity came with greater force. James came out the front door one day to find Joan yelling at the neighbor. He was horrified. The neighbors were long-time friends, and fine people. Joan was warning Mrs. Fishburn that she had evidence she was sneaking into their house late at night to steal socks, just one out of each pair. She screamed at Mrs. Fishburn, "I will no longer tolerate your intrusions! You stay out of my house and quit stealing our socks!" Mrs. Fishburn was caught off-guard. Bewildered, she looked sympathetically at James as he stood there with his mouth open and nothing to say. He put his arm around Joan and led her back into the house, where they argued for forty-five minutes about the foolishness of the accusation.

As time passed, it became impossible for James and Joan to have friends over or to attend social gatherings. Joan saw plots everywhere. No one was innocent, including her children. She also developed some compulsions. Soon there were collections of odd things stacking up in every cupboard in the house. There were boxes full of milk-bottle caps, twist ties, and the perforated clear plastic wrappings that cover lettuce; aluminum tins of all sizes were neatly arranged in the cupboards; string, ribbon, rubber bands, paper clips, and envelopes filled drawers and shelves. She began journaling obsessively, generating thousands of pages of meaningless speculation over many years. She categorized and boxed these journal pages according to subject. The compulsions entered every area of life.

The many attempts James made to obtain help for Joan proved futile. If she didn't outguess the written test, she somehow withheld her bizarre behaviors from the many psychiatrists she saw. The therapists consistently agreed that Joan was showing signs of paranoid schizophrenia, but she refused to take any medication, thinking that James was plotting with the psychiatrist to control her mind.

Disillusioned and despairing, James began to avoid Joan. He worked increasingly longer hours and left his older children to care for the younger ones in the midst of their mother's bizarre behaviors. James lived in avoidance for years. When work wasn't enough, he found hobbies to distract his attention from the pain. He was doing everything he felt he could to bring order to the chaos in his life. He would wait until 9:30 P.M. to return home because he knew she would have gone to bed right on time at 9:30.

Then one afternoon, Joan left several plastic packages stacked up on her gas stove and a fire started. Instead of taking her little girls, aged four and seven, outside the house, and calling the fire department, Joan took them into her bedroom and locked the door. Holding them in her arms, she rocked herself back and forth in a catatonic stupor. Providentially, her oldest son, Bruce, happened to arrive home from school minutes later. He ran to the hallway, grabbed the fire extinguisher and put out the fire. Already panicked, he was astounded to find his little sisters in their mother's arms in the bedroom as she continued to silently rock back and forth.

That night, Bruce explained to his father what had occurred. He pleaded with his father to be home more. This was James' wake-up call. He realized that he had been not only unfair but neglectful, burdening his oldest son with caring for the family while he was away. He now stood face-to-face with the harsh realities of Joan's mental illness. The only hope his children would have of knowing anything of a normal life would be if he separated from Joan. She was not the girl he had married.

James sought legal counsel and learned that full custody would be granted him only if he divorced Joan. He remembered his promise to stay married *for better or for worse*. He thought to himself, "That promise was made before I had children. If it were only me, I would remain in this marriage. My decision is to protect our children from danger and extreme confusion."

Sitting in the courtroom during the divorce proceedings,

James' heart was breaking. He was again asking himself, "Am I doing the right thing?" Joan had refused legal counsel and demanded to represent herself. When she was given the opportunity to speak, she began reading a document she had written which was more than sixty pages long. When she was one page into it, the judge asked her to sit down. She continued to read as if the judge had never spoken. She was warned that she would be held in contempt of court if she did not cease. She read on. The judge nodded to the bailiff, who phoned for a special psychiatric team. She continued to read. The team entered the room and attempted to gently guide her away. This was not to be. Joan began to scream and strike out at members of the team. They forced her arms behind her back and placed handcuffs on her. James laid his head on the table where he was seated. His hopes were shattered. He sobbed, grieving the loss of his mate of twenty years.

* * *

James was faced with different choices than those of Rod and Carmen:

- While Rod and Carmen could discuss their problems and empathize with each other, James and Joan could not. Joan had lost her capacity to reason, which left the responsibility solely on one partner, James.

- Because of Joan's mental illness and impaired judgment, the children were endangered. James had to make a very difficult choice when he realized that he could not allow her to be responsible for their children. While Rod and Carmen's children had to take on more responsibilities, they were not in danger.

To anticipate how you would respond if you or your spouse became mentally ill, we encourage you to discuss the following questions. While this may seem unpleasant or unnecessary, remember that the best time to discuss such a tragic possibility is now, when you both are in your "right" mind.

1. If your mate's personality changed beyond recognition, what would you do? Would you seek professional help? Would your responses be different if you had children?

2. If you were not satisfied with the professional care you received, or with the diagnosis, would you seek a second opinion?

3. How could you fulfill your promise to love "in sickness..." in the case of mental illness? Do you think James did the loving thing? Why or why not?

4. Whom would you seek for counsel? Make a tentative plan to cover the spiritual, moral, ethical, psychological, and legal dimensions of such a situation.

IN PLENTY AND IN WANT

At one of the lowest points of Dan's life, Christy made him feel like a king. He had just resigned from his position as youth director of a large church and his heart was broken to leave behind the world's greatest youth group. Dan had grown weary of the senior pastor's methods of supervision, and knew he would become bitter if he did not leave. Rather than cause division in the church, he resigned. He had not secured employment before resigning and to Dan's surprise, no job opened up. After the farewell celebration, Dan was still facing a void where a job should have been.

Mr. Anderson, the father of a high schooler in his youth group, was the general manager of a Chrysler Plymouth dealership. He had often commented on Dan's outgoing personality and how he'd make a good car salesman. He meant it as a compliment, but Dan was offended that anyone would think of him as a car salesman. But now he had no prospects of a job, so when Mr. Anderson approached him about working for him, Dan accepted the offer.

The first day he went to work feeling deeply ashamed of what he was doing. He felt sleazy and opportunistic and overbearing. The brief training he received made him feel worse, because it played off the thought that "there's a sucker born every minute." It confirmed his worst fears about what car salesmen are supposed to be and do. It was a quantum leap from church work to car sales. Dan suffered a headache and an upset stomach as he contemplated whether or not he could succeed in this new line of work and still maintain personal integrity.

When lunch came his first day on the job, Dan welcomed it like a sailor welcomes a port in a storm. Upon opening his lunch, he discovered a card and note from Christy: "Dear World, I want you to know just how proud I am of my husband." Dan read the rest of the letter and was bathed in love as Christy reached out to him, knowing how hard it was for him to work in car sales, and respecting and loving him for the gift he was giving to their family. She helped him respect himself and made the unendurable endurable. Dan felt that no dragon was too big to slay for such a woman.

* * *

For the sake of his family, Dan was willing to take a job he disliked. What turned the situation around for him was Christy's appreciation and acknowledgment of his sacrifice.

What would you do if you were faced with a similar situation? Discuss the following questions with your mate:

1. What actions would you take to support your mate in the event of a job loss?

2. If you lost your job or resigned for moral or ethical reasons, would you be willing to take an undesirable job because of your commitment to support your mate and family?

3. If your partner was discouraged, even to the point of not being motivated to look for a job, how would you encourage him or her to take a first step? How would you help your mate maintain a sense of self-respect?

A REPLY FROM THE HEART

These scenarios show that life sometimes brings unexpected twists, to which there are no easy answers. When dreams are replaced by new limitations, new plans must follow. New expectations must follow new rules.

The best place to begin is to review your commitments to God, your mate, your children, and yourself. Most of us realize that nobody promised life would be free of difficult and demanding decisions. The greatest blessing you can bring to your marriage is a commitment to your personal character and the words of your vows.

Commitment is a safety net in times of tragedy and sorrow. It is in these challenging times that the richest blessings of marriage may come—not from our situation, but from what God does with us in the situation. If ever there was a workable formula for dealing with such situations, it would be the words of the Master himself: "Do unto others as you would have them do unto you." These are the times when commitment and personal character take center stage.

A PERSONAL INVENTORY ON
INTEGRITY AND COMMITMENT

We'd like to suggest that you assess the strength of your integrity and commitment to your wedding vows. Are you doing what you said you would do? Circle *yes* or *no* for each question:

Yes No 1. Does your mate perceive that he or she is the most important person in your life?

Yes No 2. Is your mate the only person with whom you have been sexually intimate during the duration of your marriage?

Yes No 3. Do you keep small or large secrets from your mate?

Yes No 4. If you say you will do something for your mate, do you usually do it?

Yes No 5. Does your partner have *hard evidence* that he or she is cherished?

Yes No 6. Do you share confidences with other persons of the opposite sex that would hurt your mate if he or she knew?

Yes No 7. Do you get gifts from or for members of the opposite sex and not tell your mate?

Yes No 8. When your mate is ill, do you do things to comfort and make things easier for him or her?

Yes No 9. Are you better to yourself than you are to your mate?

Yes   No   10. Does your partner admire you for your integrity and your ability to keep your word?

Yes   No   11. Would your mate describe you as a kind person, especially in regard to the way you treat him or her?

Yes   No   12. Do you cherish the idea of growing old with your mate?

You can see by your answers whether or not you are keeping your vows. If you are not, you are setting your marriage up for a long fall. It takes very little effort to ruin a marriage. The formula is simple: *just break your vows.* The rest of the destruction will follow naturally. If you have broken your vows, we have good news for you. You've probably heard the saying, "Today is the first day of the rest of your life." One possible reason that God invented sleep is so that we could get things right *tomorrow.* Most mates are actually quite forgiving and will respond quickly to a positive change in negative behavior. We recommend a sincere and remorseful apology, followed immediately by deliberate positive actions. That is the most effective formula we know for turning things around.

If your vows are your priority, and you qualify as a *person of substance* in your marriage, then we applaud you! We encourage you to review this inventory from time to time, thinking of your own personal vows, the ones you took in your wedding. The goal is to look in the mirror from time to time, making sure you see the marriage partner you intended and promised to be. Then, walk away from the mirror and continue being a blessing to your mate. We think Micah 6:8 sets a beautiful tone for a person of substance:

He showed you, O man, what is good. And what does the Lord require of you? To act justly and to love mercy and to walk humbly with your God.

FOUR

Making Marriage a Priority

G od has designed a purpose for every animal on this earth. Each animal receives a daily twenty-four-hour time allotment in which to achieve that purpose; each is given a measured amount of physical and emotional energy; and each uses that time, physical energy, and emotional energy in a unique way. Elephants never sleep; bears sleep all winter; men and women sleep eight hours a day. Otters play frequently; snakes never play; humans vary widely in their amount of play.

In the animal kingdom we can see a marvelous sense of order. Rachel Carson referred to it as a "web of life." Each animal has a carefully honed purpose, whether that be to hold other animals' populations in check, to plant seeds, or to aerate the soil. Some creatures, such as roaches and flies, have the purpose of cleaning the earth, removing garbage and waste. Both humankind and animals have an assigned purpose. Animals have an ecological purpose, benefiting the earth in some specific way, whereas man does not benefit the earth ecologically except by his conscious choice to do so. We do, however, have a higher calling: to glorify God. And we fulfill that calling by keeping the priorities God has set before us. Matthew 6:33 speaks of our first and highest priority: "But seek first his kingdom and his righteousness." A brief study of the word *kingdom* shows that the word means *the sphere of God's authority*. A paraphrase might simply be, *Make God your king and live by his commands*.

In the same way he has given each of his animals an assignment, God has also given mankind an assignment. That assignment naturally unfolds in Genesis, where our history begins. What's the assignment? It is to *prioritize*:

The first priority is God.
The second priority is our relationship to our mate.
The third priority is the lives of our children.
The fourth priority is our friends.
The fifth priority is our work or career.

The career is last because it is a means to an end. Cain and Abel were both asked to use their careers to provide offerings to their first priority, the Lord God. It is always God's pattern that we use things, not people. Therefore, relationships come before work.

Our marriages have the very best chance of being happy and fulfilling if God is placed first in the lives of both partners. If only each mate were to desire the fruits of the spirit in their marriage, their relationship would be a little piece of heaven.

Galatians 5:22-23 identifies these fruits of the Spirit: "love, joy, peace, patience, kindness, goodness, faithfulness, gentleness, and self-control." These are gifts that we already possess in Christ, if he is our Savior. It is a conscious decision to exercise these wonderful character traits. Unlike the animals, who obey God instinctively, we are asked to *choose*. God sustains our joy when we choose to live in spiritual union with him.

No relationship will have greater bearing on our happiness than our marriage relationship. Because of its long-term nature, marriage could be compared to a marathon. We believe one ought to prepare for marriage as if it were a marathon.

Marathoners learn everything pertinent to the race. They must know the rules, the terrain, and the costs. The same is true for a person entering into marriage. Marathoners must train for the race, or they will never complete it. It's not something you can physically achieve without committing months to training. It will require a combination of time and sacrifice and practice. People who approach marriage with a less dedicated attitude make a fatal assumption. That false assumption currently leads to the death of 67 percent of the marriages attempted in America.

Marathoners must also know the route. In the 1994 Boston Marathon, a runner took a wrong turn. He was in first place, and only got off course ten yards, but that ten yards almost cost him the race. Knowing where you are going, and setting personal goals, can make all the difference in the world toward success in your marriage.

Marathoners must set a pace they can sustain. If they go too fast, they will tire before the end of the race; if they go too slow, they will fall behind the other runners. There is a pace to marriage as well, a graceful consistency which brings you to the end of the line with style and merit. Finding the rhythm is what this book is about. Has your marriage been given its rightful place as the second priority in your life, with only God ahead of it?

GOOD NEWS, BAD NEWS

Jessica pulled off the interstate at the Mt. Hermon exit. Her commute was forty miles into San Jose, where she was employed by Technonet, a large, expanding software company in Silicon Valley. She was the sales representative for an area including San Jose, Oakland, and San Francisco. She was the company's rising star in sales. Her accomplishments had caught the attention of the company's president, Bob Haller. He wanted his other sales representatives to grasp her methods and catch her enthusiasm for Technonet's products.

Haller strategized a plan to make Jessica his national sales manager. It would be awkward, because she would have to supervise several people who had previously supervised her. It also meant a $25,000-per-year raise and would require a great deal of travel—as much as three weeks per month, with the option of coming home or staying in hotels on weekends.

Jessica was overwhelmed with mixed emotions. Who could have dreamed that she would be experiencing this kind of promotion this early in her career? On the other hand, accepting the position would mean sacrificing time with her husband, Jeremy.

Jessica expressed her appreciation to Bob Haller for his confidence. "Thank you, Bob, for choosing me to represent Technonet. I am deeply complimented by your trust in my abilities, especially knowing what an able sales team we have. I feel, however, that I need to talk to Jeremy about the scope of this decision. How soon do you need my answer?"

Bob Haller laughed and said, "As usual, I'd like it yesterday! But I'll give you a week. Let me know after the sales meeting on Wednesday."

On the drive home, Jessica sorted through the many implications of accepting the promotion. The decision would affect Jeremy as much as it would her. It would require a thorough discussion and a joint decision.

Jessica sat down immediately to a well-prepared meal. Tuesday was Jeremy's night to cook and he was quite the chef, having perfected his culinary talents during college and bachelor days.

"Guess what, Jeremy? Bob Haller called me into his office today. And I can't believe what he had to say. He offered me a promotion. And it's very impressive. I couldn't get home fast enough to tell you about it!"

Jeremy looked delighted, knowing what excellent work his wife performed for the company. "Sounds exciting!"

Jessica smiled and said teasingly, "Jeremy, this is a good news, bad news story. The good news is there's a $25,000 pay raise!"

Jeremy couldn't contain himself. He whistled a cheer!

Jessica continued, "It also means a prestigious new title: national sales manager!" Again, Jeremy was thrilled to think of his wife receiving such a fabulous advance in her career.

"That's fantastic, Jessica! So, what's the bad news?"

"The bad news involves time and travel. Lots of it. Too much of it. So much of it that accepting the position is out of the question. But, before I turn it down, I want to talk over the details with you. I want your input."

Jeremy looked surprised. "Jessica, you must be talking about a lot of travel. What are we looking at here? A few days a month? Once a week?"

"Three weeks per month on the road. Three weeks without eating dinner with you. Three weeks of phone contact only, unless I fly home on weekends. Three weeks of sleeping alone. Jeremy, I'm not doing it! You're too important to me. Our marriage is everything. We would become strangers. Think of it!"

Spontaneously Jeremy reached across the table and squeezed her hand. "Jessica, I love you. To think you would give up a position of this importance for our marriage confirms all the things I've always believed about you! I want you to know that I would have supported you no matter what. I admit that the thought of your being gone three weeks a month is truly painful. If I should ever be asked to disrupt our plans due to a job opportunity, I'll remember this moment and your sense of priorities. How do you think Bob Haller will take the news of your decision to decline the promotion?"

Jessica shrugged. "Hard to say. He may not understand our priorities toward each other. On the other hand, he's thrilled with my sales figures. I won't worry about it." She felt relieved. She knew all along she would not take the position of national sales manager, because it did not fit into the plans she and Jeremy were making for their lives together.

In the end, Jessica's supervisor became national sales manager, Jessica was promoted to regional sales manager, and

Jessica and Jeremy continued to give their marriage its rightful priority.

Was Jessica right to give such high priority to her marriage? We think so, and it's our prayer that you will, too.

MARRIAGE INVENTORY

The following questions will help you determine how you are doing at prioritizing your marriage. Discuss your answers with your partner.

Marriage

1. Do you feel that you have kept the promises you made at the altar?

2. Have you loved your mate "in sickness and in health, in plenty and in want, for richer and for poorer"?

3. Do you think the best of your partner?

4. Do you derive pleasure from mutual involvements? Part of making marriage a priority is setting goals together. (See appendix C, on goal-setting.)

5. Do you wish to achieve a common good between you?

6. Do you enjoy your mate's pleasure more than your own?

7. Do you carve out time and save energy for encounters with your partner, including conversation, affection, lovemaking, activities, tasks, and projects?

8. Do you consider your mate when you make important decisions that will affect him or her?

Children

1. Have you done something measurable and observable to show that your children are a priority... more than other family and friends, more than your career and hobbies?

2. What exactly have you done?

Extended family

1. What have you done to show that you value your extended family?

2. What have you done to maintain the bonds with these significant people?

Friends

1. What evidence is there that your mate has been given priority treatment above your friends and the activities you enjoy with them?

2. Are you as enthusiastic about spending time with your mate as you are about spending time with your friends? Or have you slipped into complacency, taking your mate for granted and reserving your best social behavior for others?

Career

1. How have you set boundaries in your career involvements to give your marriage top priority?

2. Have you been successful in balancing your career responsibilities with your marital commitments?

Following is a list of common negative choices in the area of making marriage a priority. Review each and discuss these with your mate. Notice how destructive these behaviors are to a marriage. If you have fallen into these traps, free yourself as soon as possible by setting new priorities.

1. Have you become self-indulgent—especially with finances, friends, interests, or work? What specific steps can you take to turn this around? (See appendix B, "How Do We Plan a Budget?" for practical instruction.)

2. Have you broken promises, either through outright lying or by omitting important details? What do you need to do to clear up the deception, so that you can promote honesty in your marriage?

3. Have you become a master at dragging others down—especially your mate, but also your children, parents, or in-laws? What can you do to *encourage* your mate (and others)? How can you begin to enhance your relationship?

4. Have you been insensitive, demanding, or vengeful? (This may pertain to your mate in the areas of emotions, intimacy, and his or her priorities.) Are you willing to apologize and start trying to be more considerate, working together so that each of you can get your needs met?

5. Have you been irresponsible or forgetful toward your partner? What do you want to do to turn that around? Are there tasks to which you have committed yourself but have not done? How can you add them to your schedule and fulfill your promises?

6. Have you been disloyal? Have you convinced some neighbors, friends, or colleagues of your good reasons for disloyalty? Have they become advocates for you, if not accomplices with you? You have an opportunity to set the record straight by apologizing to your partner and clearing things up with your friends.

Making your marriage a priority is a serious and worthy endeavor. It is a lofty and regal pursuit. Thankfully, it is also a pursuit that has room for lots of fun! In fact, we can say beyond a shadow of a doubt that you cannot hope to attain most of what God has intended for you in marriage without arranging your life with the following priorities:

God
Your mate
Your children
Your relatives
Your friends
Your career (and hobbies, interests, etc.)

We hope we have sufficiently underscored the importance of making marriage a priority, and that you have gained helpful insights from reviewing your own priorities. We encourage you to make any changes that will order your life God's way. You and your partner will benefit greatly from that choice!

FIVE

Building Trust

The Story Told

Sam got out of his Toyota pickup, sighed, and looked at the small rented house he had lived in for five years with his wife, Linda. Today he had the unenviable task of bringing bad news to Linda. This was not unusual for Sam; the choices he made and the way he lived away from home created many baskets of bad news.

As Sam opened the door, Linda was there to greet him. She was always there. When Sam said he didn't deserve Linda, it was one of the few times that he clearly spoke the truth.

"Hi, Sam!" Linda said with enthusiasm, kissing him on the cheek. "Tell me about your day."

Sam, avoiding eye contact, began, "It wasn't a great day, Linda. Jim Higgins, that boss I was telling you about—who was so jealous of my

The Rest of the Story

Sam and Linda were never able to accumulate enough money for a down payment, mainly due to Sam's sporadic employment. Sam had a habit of showing up late for work, leaving jobs uncompleted, and blaming his coworkers. He took excessively long breaks, and sometimes even left the job site with no explanation. In seven years he had never once failed to claim every day of his sick leave. He was known for having a chip on his shoulder, and for arguing with his supervisor and coworkers.

Jim Higgins was a thoughtful and fair-minded supervisor. He was not jealous of Sam. On accomplishments—fired me today. He made up a bunch of lies about me, and told the owner. I tried to get an appointment to talk to the owner, but I guess Jim lied so good that I was just told there was no need to meet. Sometimes it don't pay to work your head off, when they go and treat you like this!"

This was not the first time Linda had heard such a story. In five short years she had heard similar lines seven times. She loved Sam, and chose to believe him. There were times when she wondered if there was a real story beyond the story she was told. But Linda was the kind of wife who simply believes because she simply loves. It would become increasingly more difficult to love so simply, but for now she just held Sam in her arms and told him it was going to be alright.

Sam handled the family finances. He had become a master at juggling late payments, and at writing letters to creditors and obtaining more than his share of grace.

Linda asked innocently, "Sam, are we going to make it?"

Sam looked directly at her and said, "Now, one of the reasons I take care of the checkbook is so you don't have to worry. We're doing fine."

the contrary, it was his habit to help everyone under his authority to succeed. No less than ten times he had encouraged Sam to improve his work and be a team player. Even with Sam's horrible track record, Jim was genuinely upset about having to fire him for incompetence and insubordination. When Sam protested, Jim offered him the opportunity to speak to the owner of the business, but Sam cursed and declined the offer, choosing instead to storm off with paycheck in hand.

Sam was given severance pay, but never told Linda; they didn't have a dime in savings. He used the severance pay to buy a hunting rifle—which he kept hidden. He later asked Linda to borrow money from her parents to temporarily cover living expenses until he could get his new business started.

Linda knew better than to ask more. On some occasions, not knowing had given her a measure of comfort.

Sam sat down and turned on the television. Turning to Linda, he added, "I'm really glad I took those special classes when I got my electrician's license. It'll make getting a new job a breeze. Linda, if you don't mind, I don't want to talk about this too much. Thinkin' about what Jim did to me makes me angry. It just ain't fair. I don't want to take it out on you and the kids. So, let's just drop it, okay?"

"This just isn't right! I want to call Jim and set him straight!" exclaimed Linda.

"Thanks, Linda, but I don't want to talk about it anymore tonight."

Linda replied, "Let's just say you quit 'cause you didn't want to work for that jerk anyway."

Linda went into the kitchen and called her mother. "Guess what, Mom? Remember Jim Higgins, Sam's boss? He got jealous of Sam again and Sam decided he would just quit. I guess Jim was threatened because Sam was a better electrician than he was. Sometimes life isn't fair, is it, Mom?"

Linda's mother agreed, but thought to herself that her son-in-

Linda wanted to hide Sam's tarnished track record from her parents, children, and friends. She said he had quit, hoping that no questions would be asked.

law had certainly had quite a number of jobs—and run-ins with bosses. But being supportive, she just expressed her concern.

Sam wandered into the kitchen and pulled a soda out of the refrigerator. Popping the tab, he told Linda to tell her mother that he was tired of working for someone else for low pay. "I'm just gonna start my own business—Sam's Electric. I'll have ten trucks in no time. Then I can do the hiring and firing." His voice faded as he walked back to the den to watch "Hawaii 5-0."

Sam had never taken special electrician courses. He didn't achieve his goal of becoming a licensed contractor, and he cheated on his journeyman's license test. He just didn't have the self-discipline needed to be a contractor or run his own business. After four months of unemployment, Sam resumed his pattern of moving from job to job, always covering up his inadequacies. He continued to hide his true feelings and refused to grow in his knowledge or practice of the truth. Linda continued the journey with Sam, knowing quietly in her heart that something major was missing from their relationship.

Trust is foundational to marriage, and truth is the paramount foundation of trust. The Scriptures reveal the tremendous value of truth.

I have no greater joy than to hear that my children are walking in the truth.   3 John 4

Nowhere is truth more essential than in marriage. It has been said that love is giving as much as we know of ourselves to as much as we know of our mate. Statements and actions of truth develop into trust. And trust is the glue that bonds two people. An unyielding commitment to truth builds a stronghold for an enduring marriage.

There are numerous benefits to telling the truth:

1. *People who tell the truth* enjoy the deep and growing respect of their mate, children, friends and family, colleagues and employers.

2. *People who tell the truth* are entrusted with greater and more meaningful levels of responsibility.

3. *People who tell the truth* are sought out for advice and direction.

4. *People who tell the truth* have the light and airy feeling of a clear conscience. Their back is never bowed by the cumbersome weight of guilt. Their mind is free from the tangled chaos of anxiety created by lying.

5. *People who tell the truth* are free to use their energy and creativity to live well, to fulfill their purpose and to maximize their relationships.

6. *People who tell the truth* can be confident that they enjoy the approval of God.

7. *Couples who tell the truth in marriage* live in the constant glow of knowing they and their mate are trustworthy.

8. *Couples who tell the truth in marriage* create comfort and security for each other instead of doubt and distrust.

If such benefits can be had just by telling the truth, why do we lie? Why do we lie to ourselves, to God, and to each other?

1. *We lie to gain acceptance.* Sam told Linda that his boss was the culprit, so that his own behavior might continue to appear acceptable to his wife.

2. *We lie to avoid conflict.* By calling for silence and lying about their financial state, Sam was able to avoid conflict and pain.

3. *We lie to injure others intentionally.* Through lying, Sam injured the reputation of Jim Higgins, not only to his wife but to anyone else who heard the story.

4. *We lie for personal gain.* Sam lied about his severance pay so that he might buy the rifle.

5. *We lie to build up our pride.* Sam lied to Linda for reasons of pride, by making himself the head of an imaginary company.

FORMS AND DEGREES OF LIES

There are no innocent lies. "White" lies are the building blocks that bear the weight of dark and evil lies. Although it is true that one lie can do more damage than another, it may also be true that any lie is equally damaging to the liar. Lies perpetuate lies. They are their own Pandora's box.

Lies could be classified into several categories:

1. **Extreme exaggeration.** Exaggeration warps perspective. It makes something considerably larger or smaller, more important or less important than it ought to be. It renders one unable to deal properly within the realm of reality in order to solve a problem—for the solutions themselves will be exaggerations.

2. **Delusions of grandeur.** A sad form of lying, delusions of grandeur indicate that the deluded person feels very inadequate. They need to say things about themselves that are not true in order to gain the perception of equal footing with the person to whom they are speaking. When their lie is exposed, the very goal they wished to achieve is destroyed, and they find themselves descending to a lower plane.

3. **The cover-up.** When we cover up for a friend, we become co-conspirators in the lie. Really good friends will help their closest friends face the truth and bear the consequences. Good friends refuse to participate in the destructive practice of lying.

4. **White lies.** The white lie is to lying as marijuana is to heroin, the first step in a downward spiral.

5. **"Gray" areas.** People may feel more freedom to lie in gray areas, convincing themselves they are not really lying. "If in

doubt, don't," is a wise axiom and can keep us out of much trouble.

6. **Lying for profit.** Any time that we lie for profit, it will be at someone else's expense. Any given economy has limited funds; when we profit untruthfully, someone else loses. No wonder the Scripture warns against ill-gotten gain. We need to be careful as couples when we fill out tax forms, insurance or credit applications, or any financial documents that provide privileges and opportunities. The availability of such privileges and opportunities assume our personal integrity.

7. **"Promises, promises."** Gain a reputation for being a person of your word. Gary enjoyed sixteen years of life with a father who was a man of his word. At the graveside service, Gary was besieged by many men who had known and loved his father. Every one of them addressed the issue of his father's integrity—something Gary had seen all of his life: "Your dad was a man of his word. No contract was as binding as your dad's handshake. If he said he'd do it, he'd do it. If he said he'd be there at 5:00 A.M., he was there at 5:00 A.M. If he said he'd do it for $50, he did it for $50 even if it cost him $60. They don't make men like your dad anymore." What a legacy Gary's father left him by his wonderful example of integrity!

Lies create traps. Lies lead to more lies to cover the former lie. We soon lose track of reality. For some, it leads to mental illness. For others, it just leads to eroding relationships. Mark Twain once quipped, "No one has a good enough memory to be a good liar." Simply telling the truth in any and every situation is excellent advice to give or receive.

TRANSFORMING THROUGH TRUTH

Let's revisit the story of Sam and Linda, revising it to reflect an unyielding commitment to truth. We will see the transforming nature of truth in the lives of a couple who had become entrenched in lies.

Sam got out of his Toyota pickup, sighed and looked at the small rented house he had lived in for five years with his wife, Linda. He had the unenviable task of bringing bad news to a wife who deserved much better. Sam thought to himself, *This is the seventh job I've messed up in five years. Something has got to change and it's gonna have to start with me. It can't always be everyone else's fault. Jim Higgins warned me at least ten times that I needed to turn my life around. I don't even know where to begin. He was a good boss and I should have listened to him.*

Sam opened the screen door. Tears welled up in his eyes as his wife appeared. Linda held him close in her arms and said lovingly, "Sam, what's wrong?"

Sam choked out, "Everything, everything."

Linda replied, "Tell me what happened."

Burdened, Sam walked to the couch and sat down, placing his head in both hands. "I'll tell you what happened, Linda. The same thing that happens every year about this time. I blew a perfectly good job. Jim Higgins warned me over and over that, if I didn't get it together, he'd have to let me go. Linda, I hate to admit it, but I didn't get it together. Not in my last six jobs, and now not in this one."

Linda sat next to her husband and put her hand on his shoulder. "What did Jim want you to do?"

Sam turned to her and said, "Just what I was supposed to do. Just what anyone would be expected to do. Check my work for mistakes, get it done on time, take reasonable breaks, and treat people like human beings."

Linda protested, "But, Sam, you always do that. What are you talking about?"

"Linda, I've been living a lie. I've been hassling everyone, blaming everyone, and basically making a jerk out of myself. For a long time. Then I've come home and pretended the problems were all theirs. I can't even tell the difference anymore."

"How are we doing financially?" Linda asked.

Sam pulled a check from his dusty jeans, "This is my last paycheck. Plus I got two weeks severance pay. We're gonna have to be really careful with this money because we don't have much in the bank and this can go real quick if we're not careful. Linda, there's something I've gotta do right now to face up to the truth. I'll be back in a couple of hours. I've gotta go talk to Jim."

"Are you gonna ask for your job back? Will he give you another chance?" she asked with her voice cracking.

"No, Linda. I don't deserve to get my job back. But he's a nice guy. And I think he'll tell me the truth about how to keep the next job I get, so this doesn't keep happening. At least, I hope he'll talk to me. See you later."

When Sam got to the job site, Jim looked confused, but extended his hand warmly as Sam offered a handshake. Sam spoke humbly and said, "Jim, I don't know why you kept me as long as you did. I didn't deserve it. And I want you to know I'm not here to get my job back. It's just that it dawned on me when I was driving home that I need to learn what to do to keep jobs in the future. I know you told me before, but my attitude wasn't any good and I didn't really listen. Well, I'm ready to listen now. If you would write down some pointers for me, I'd sure appreciate it."

Jim put his arm around Sam and said, "Sure, buddy. Let's go for it."

Jim covered everything from attitude to excellence of work, and assured Sam he believed that he could be a great electrician for someone. Sam didn't get his job back, but that day he took an important step which kept him employed for the next eleven years. His honesty carried over to his marriage. Never again was Linda the last to know if there was a problem in Sam's life. She had taken first place, the first to know and the first to be trusted.

A PERSONAL INVITATION FOR
QUIET CONTEMPLATION

Many Old Testament proverbs contrast the path of truth with the perilous path of falsehood. Below is a collection of these wise sayings from the book of Proverbs. How might each of these apply to your own life?

A wholesome tongue is a tree of life,
but perverseness in it breaks the spirit.
Proverbs 15:4 (NKJV)

A truthful witness does not deceive,
but a false witness pours out lies.   **14:5**

A truthful witness saves lives,
but a false witness is deceitful.   **14:25**

The tongue of the wise commends knowledge,
but the mouth of the fool gushes folly.   **15:2**

He who speaks truth declares righteousness,
But a false witness, deceit.   **12:17 (NKJV)**

Do they not go astray who devise evil?
But mercy and truth belong to those who devise good.
14:22 (NKJV)

Let not mercy and truth forsake you;
Bind them around your neck,
Write them on the tablet of your heart,
And so find favor and high esteem in the sight of God and
man.   **3:3-4 (NKJV)**

He who conceals his sins does not prosper,
but whoever confesses and renounces them finds mercy.
                                              28:13

Quietly consider areas where you might revive your convictions and enhance your code of conduct to reflect greater truthfulness. What a valuable asset to contribute to any relationship!

SIX

Staying Inside the Lines: Establishing Boundaries

When Gary worked at the Los Angeles Zoo, he had to come to grips with beautiful wild animals being kept in cages. Being a naturalist at heart, at first it seemed restrictive and unnatural to him. As the years went by, it dawned on him that the cages the animals lived in protected them from predators, not to mention thoughtless zoo patrons. The animals couldn't get lost, they would never suffer from drought or famine, and they were very available for medical attention should they need it. Because of the boundaries established for the animals, they were far more healthy and lived a good deal longer than they would have lived in the wild.

Although animals at the zoo have no choice concerning boundaries, we humans do. If we choose to set wise boundaries within our marriages, we will enjoy a degree of protection from predators. There were occasions at the zoo when mated animals had to be separated for a time so they wouldn't hurt each other. We hope to describe boundaries that will keep marital partners from hurting each other as well.

FIVE ESSENTIAL BOUNDARIES
FOR MARRIAGE PARTNERS

1. **Appropriate contact with members of the opposite sex.**
Prior to marriage there was no particular need to limit contact with the opposite sex. Now, things are different. What

85

was acceptable for a single person can present danger for a married person. Overly friendly behavior toward the opposite sex sends the message that you are available and shopping. Marriage carries with it no particular magic that keeps us from noticing and desiring people now forbidden to us. So, it is important that we take the responsibility to set our own personal boundaries, to protect us from the inappropriate desires of others and from our own inappropriate desires toward them.

Surely this is the kind of thing Jesus had in mind when he taught us to pray, "Lead us not into temptation, but deliver us from the evil one" (Matthew 6:13). At the zoo Gary learned that, if you're not near the germ, you can't catch the disease. There is great danger in spending time with a member of the opposite sex in a private setting. All of us are vulnerable to temptation; no one is exempt. It is our personal responsibility to protect our vulnerability by making choices that minimize the exposure. In practical terms, don't go out to eat together, don't travel together, don't indulge in any type of private times together. On occasion, business and other projects may require exclusive and extended contact with the opposite sex. It is each partner's responsibility to inform the other, to minimize the contact, and to make careful choices about conduct during those times.

2. **Appropriate subject matter when communicating with others.** The goal of appropriate communication with others is to protect your mate and your marriage. Discussing matters that would belittle, embarrass, humiliate, or violate confidences between you and your mate is off-limits. Never entertain questions from others which evaluate your mate in a personal way. Do not reveal intimate details of your sexual behavior. Do not break confidences. Communicate with others as if your mate were present. Use words that edify, affirm, and promote. Be willing to say, "That is a private matter. I would not be comfortable discussing that."

With the opposite sex, don't communicate in ways that would promote a strong emotional involvement, arouse sexual feelings, or promote intimacy. Flirtation is quite different from friendliness. We all recognize the difference. If you overstep the line, apologize to the person and to your partner.

3. **Schedule time together.** Consult with each other frequently concerning whether either of you is spending too much time away from your marriage. In this area, there is a varying tolerance level for each couple. Whereas some couples—those in the armed services, for instance—may have learned to cope with long separations, other couples suffer in a matter of days when deprived of contact. It is important to discuss this often.

Schedules and responsibilities change regularly. It is essential that partners assess their commitments and agree about time usage. Sometimes this requires some negotiating of the schedules and even *reserving future time to spend together*. As a rule, marriages are best served when there is quantity and quality time devoted to the relationship. We suggest you work together to protect your marriage from neglect by scheduling time in a way that says your marriage is a top priority. As far as we know, no one has ever been heard screaming in their last breath, "I wish I'd spent more hours at the office!"

4. **Agree on your use of community property and finances.** Other chapters in this book address the matter of priorities, control, and finances. If you simply keep in mind that your marriage is a divine partnership, you will stay inside the lines, respecting the right of your mate to participate as an equal with you in the use of your property and funds. There will be an ongoing need for communication, updates, planning, and goals in this area. Couples can derive tremendous

satisfaction from the unity they enjoy in dealing together with their material needs and wants. This kind of teamwork yields many long-term benefits.

Living within the lines of an agreed-upon budget will be the best boundary you can establish here.

5. Agree on strategies for rearing children. Because each partner grew up in a different family, setting goals and working within the lines is essential in child-rearing. It will allow you to create a united front as parents, so that your children will respect your leadership and receive consistent input that doesn't contradict or confuse.

What about discipline? What will you as a married couple do when your children behave in a certain way? You must decide if spanking is an alternative. You must determine degrees of discipline. You will need to agree about your children's rules regarding bedtimes, diet, homework, social activities, extracurricular activities, educational plans, standards for appearance, hygiene, and daily responsibilities.

Perhaps you have limited parenting skills. If you find that, even when you work together, your children are still more of a challenge than you can manage, we recommend that you investigate the availability of parenting classes, or books or videos on parenting. Focus on the Family always offers tremendous resources. Their address is: Focus on the Family, P.O. Box 1800, Colorado Springs, CO 80995.

EQUIPPED WITH A PLAN

Garrett heard a light tap on his office door. "Come in!" he called out in his usual hospitable tone. The door opened and in walked Erin Tremain. She was breathtakingly beautiful, and all too available. Garrett felt a wave of discomfort being alone in his office with Erin—even with the door opened. He wondered why she was there, because their responsibilities at Chicago Fund Life Insurance Company did not overlap. There was no apparent business reason for her visit.

"Erin, how can I help you?" he asked. She sat down on the edge of his desk with a flirtatious posture.

"Oh, I was just looking to get out of the cold."

Garrett, not picking up the cue, asked if there was something wrong with the air-conditioning. Erin laughed, "You're so innocent, Garrett. You're really a nice guy, aren't you? Your wife is so lucky to have found you. Does she know what she has?"

"I'm really a lot of trouble, but I think she loves me, if that's what you mean. I'm still concerned about your being cold," he continued.

"Oh, that!" she said. "I was referring to life. I've been feeling very lonely lately with nobody to talk to but my Shitzu, Babbette. And she's hardly enough to keep my feet warm."

Garrett felt flushed, and noticed his tie feeling tight. "I guess divorce can be really tough. I'm sorry to hear you're having a rough time."

Erin glanced at her watch and proclaimed, "It's lunch time, Garrett. I came down to ask you to join me for lunch. I'm buying."

Garrett did not hesitate, "Erin, I must thank you for your offer, but I really can't accept. Sally and I have an agreement. It goes like this. Under no conditions do we dine with people of the opposite sex alone—married or unmarried. No offense to you personally. We just built this into our marriage as a safeguard seventeen years ago. So far, our agreement has served us well. But thanks for the invitation."

Erin looked impressed. "That's a good plan. If my ex-husband and I had made that plan, we'd probably still be together. That's probably one reason I came into your office. I wanted to be close to someone that has these kinds of values. So tell me, Garrett, where does a woman like me go to find a man like you?"

Feeling complimented, Garrett said, "Thank you for the kind words, Erin. I honestly think there are lots of good guys around, and you won't have any trouble at all attracting them. I suspect the key will be setting some good boundaries and appropriate expectations that you are willing to wait for. Just between you and me, there's a guy named Rick Caldwell up in marketing who seems to be open to dating. I don't know if you're open to it, but I'd be willing to introduce you. If you wish, I'll touch base with him and see what we can put together. Are you interested?"

Erin nodded affirmatively and winked. "Who would turn down an offer like that? Like I told you, I'm tired of my Shitzu!"

That evening, Garrett sat down on the couch next to Sally and said, "Guess what? You're never going to believe this. A beautiful woman from the investments division paid me a visit today. It wasn't a business meeting. She had an agenda and I was it!" Garrett proceeded to tell Sally the details of the encounter, and how he handled the matter. He assured Sally that he would be on the alert for her future moves, each time setting clear boundaries, and each time keeping Sally posted. That was their mutual agreement for protecting against the predator of adultery.

* * *

The excellent example that Garrett and Sally illustrate is the ability to establish boundaries and successfully stay inside the lines. Not only did they have good sexual boundaries, but they were well established in the way they scheduled their time, how they spent their money, and how they handled confidential information. The by-product of good boundaries was the great joy of living in a completely safe atmosphere of marriage. They created that atmosphere and guarded it faithfully.

Staying inside the lines builds security into your marital relationship. It will protect you from predators, it will build trust, and it will promote understanding and intimacy. Couples who know the fine art of planning and honoring boundaries find that they have more freedom, not less. What may once have been perceived as a cage can now be viewed as armor.

We must determine appropriate times and places for everything in our marriage. That process is what we call boundary setting. The assignment is given at the altar. What God has put together, let no man separate (Matthew 19:6). Your marriage is worth protecting. We encourage you to take the assignment seriously, so that you can enjoy an enriched marriage for a lifetime. See the "Recommended Reading" list for further information about boundaries.

SEVEN

A Journey into Deepening Friendship: Developing Intimacy

E laine sat in the comfort of her family room and smiled. She thought to herself, "Two weeks and we will have been married for twelve years." She reflected that saying "I do" to Rich was one of the greatest decisions of her life. Elaine seemed to be naturally adept at relationships and had at least five *best* girlfriends to show for it. She enjoyed the kind of friendships that allowed her the freedom to bare her heart without a second thought. The joy that she was feeling at this very moment came from the knowledge that she now had this kind of relationship with her husband. She realized also that Rich had traveled a long road to come to the point where she could honestly call him her *very* best friend.

In the beginning months of their marriage, Rich was private and inward about his deepest feelings. But he had changed. It didn't just happen suddenly. Early on in the marriage, he determined that he wanted to be an excellent husband. One day he asked Elaine, "What do you need from me more than anything else?" *That is a wonderful question to ask your mate!* Elaine responded that she most needed to know in her heart that they were very best friends. He smiled and said, "No problem. That's what I want, too."

Elaine never purchased a single book on marriage to give to Rich. She didn't need to. He bought them! She knew that he was internalizing the best of what he was reading, because she saw the evidence emerge in his behavior toward her. First, she noticed that it began to be natural for Rich to take her hand when they were watching a movie or strolling through a mall. Reinforcing this gentle attention, she would comment, "I like that." Rich answered, "I read in a book somewhere that women like that from the man in their life. And I guess the book was right." Then he added, "I like it, too!"

She also noted that Rich grew in his ability to listen, even to the point that he would voluntarily switch off the TV when they were talking about something important. This always reaffirmed to Elaine her priority position in Rich's life. Their talking was frequent. Conversing daily, really conversing, Elaine and Rich grew to know, beyond a shadow of a doubt, each other's current dreams and disappointments. Elaine's intimate disclosures to Rich had never come back to haunt her through breach of confidence. Rich had also learned that Elaine thrived by knowing she was esteemed by him. Harsh and critical language was now absent from their interactions, even during conflict and disagreement. He never gave Elaine the feeling that he was simply waiting for a chance to make a point, but instead let her know that she was entirely heard and understood.

While Elaine was in the family room thanking God for her marriage, Rich, an architect, was driving to the job site of his most recent project. He uttered a silent prayer, "Thank you, God, for the gift of Elaine. She has always been there for me, patient to let me grow into the kind of husband she deserved to have from the first day." As he drove, Rich recalled a parade of wonderful memories of his marriage. Certain memories lingered as he scanned the twelve-year panorama. He was struck by the realization that Elaine always looked so happy to see him come home. He loved that she often made dinner a romantic event. On dozens of occasions, he had opened his mail at work only to discover an encouraging or lighthearted note ending with, "All my love, Elaine." She made Christmas, Thanksgiving, Easter, birthdays, and even routine days wonderfully special.

Rich appreciated that Elaine respected him as a person and as a man. He was very thankful that Elaine could be trusted in every level of her behavior. He liked knowing that he would always hear the truth from her—the truth about her and the truth about him. Such honesty was spoken in love, in kind words and tones, even when critical. If he had to pick one moment out of the twelve years of their marriage to define what he most loved about Elaine, it would have been a moment shared over a very painful event. In the course of Rich's first job, his company had downsized. His lack of seniority made him the logical target for cutbacks. Rejected, he returned home wanting to inform Elaine in person. Driving home, he felt shame and humiliation and inadequacy. The initial sting was among the most painful experiences of Rich's life. As he started to explain that he had been fired from his job, he began to weep uncontrollably. Elaine rushed to him and held him for the longest time. No words were necessary. Her strong embrace was ample evidence of her deep caring. When he was able to articulate his disappointment and humiliation, she expressed that she understood and that she was not in the least bit afraid of their future. In her own sincere way, she expressed her faith that someone would soon recognize Rich's real value and hire him.

Even in that first painful evening, Rich experienced some optimism that he still had something worthwhile to give the world of architecture. Elaine did not waver in her encouragement, although it seemed to Rich an endless five months until he again found employment. He remembered how many times Elaine just kissed and held him, telling him how proud she was to be his wife. He would always be grateful for this memory, when it had seemed that she alone believed in him.

Rich and Elaine were both good at planning surprises for each other and setting aside time and savings for intimate and romantic getaways. The getaways allowed the opportunity to linger over candle-lit meals, take long walks, and communicate at the deepest level, heart-to-heart. Rich and Elaine had what most couples could have, but choose not to. They had a deep and intimate relationship.

* * *

Intimacy results from the presence of several specific factors. Let's define intimacy in light of the story we have just shared. What made the difference for this real-life (yes!) couple?

THE TOP TEN FACTORS FOR ACHIEVING INTIMACY

1. **Attitude of love.** First and foremost, intimacy is nurtured by a consistent and loving attitude. Characteristic of that love is a constant desire to uphold your mate's sense of value. Rich read marriage books to become a better husband, and in so doing, demonstrated to Elaine her worth.

   Elaine, for her part, expressed confidence in Rich when he could no longer be confident in himself. Focusing on his character, she looked beyond the moment.

2. **Atmosphere of safety.** Of great importance is the feeling that the failures and successes of your life will be received by your partner with joy and support, though the workplace, the extended family, and your circle of friends may turn on you. Can you picture Rich in the arms of Elaine, experiencing support and acceptance in his moment of grief? Can you share Elaine's joy when Rich repeatedly kept confidences that she shared with him? There was a refuge in their relationship.

3. **Abundant and intimate communication.** Taking the time to share everything, from the mundane to the deeply personal and spiritual aspects of our lives, is essential for

achieving intimacy. Sometimes it's the things we *say*, sometimes it's the things we *do*. In Rich and Elaine's story, we saw Rich's commitment to communication when he turned off the television to talk with his wife. We saw Elaine's when she listened to Rich's grief.

4. **Intimacy is a process, not an event.** As couples we must be patient as we grow in the area of intimacy. It is a slow process of *giving as much as we know of ourselves to as much as we know of our mate*. It was refreshing to see Elaine's patience as she watched Rich gain relationship skills that were new to him, but so natural to her. It was equally refreshing to see Rich take the initiative to educate himself to the worthy cause of marital maturity.

5. **It isn't doing things together, it's being things together.** There is nothing more empty than a busy schedule. Just being involved in an active lifestyle together does not necessarily generate intimacy. The ability to enjoy your mate no matter what you are doing will build intimacy. Elaine and Rich enjoyed getaways, but just being together at home, doing tasks around the house, was also satisfying.

6. **It takes two people to be intimate.** Intimacy flows back and forth between two people, giving and taking. It cannot exist alone. If Elaine were impatient for deeper intimacy early in the marriage, she may have stopped the process Rich had begun, of becoming a more loving and intimate husband. Instead, Elaine helped Rich in his efforts. Her patience and appreciation surely kept Rich craving a deeper relationship with her.

7. **Complete disclosure.** If anyone hopes to become intimate with his or her mate, there can be no secrets. If you keep from revealing your true self, you will be inviting your

mate to love someone else. He or she will miss out on the *real* you, with all the positive and less than positive characteristics. Not only do we need to be honest about ourselves, we also need to be honest about our feelings toward each other. To be intimate means to say the difficult thing that will help your mate to grow, or to take the risk of sharing a hurt so that future changes can improve the relationship.

If we think what we have to say might injure our mate's self-esteem or cause them to think poorly of us, it is important to express those fears. For example, say, "I believe that what I have to say is necessary for us to grow. If I withhold this, I believe I am hurting our relationship." If the disclosure is actually a negative opinion about the partner or something the partner does, it is important to say, "I am telling you this in hopes that I can support you in getting a better outcome in the future"; or, "I am telling you this because otherwise you won't know it bothers me, and you won't consider making a change." A gentle attitude makes all the difference. Rich's willingness to cry in Elaine's arms gave her the opportunity to know the depth of his anguish, and gave him the opportunity to be truly comforted and supported.

8. **Enthusiastically accepting your mate exactly as is.** If a relationship is to be intimate, it will flourish under the gentle rain of approval. Appreciation, encouragement, and affirmation will draw you and your mate toward intimacy. When Elaine held Rich in her arms, and assured him of his worth by looking ahead to his future employment, she affirmed who he was and what he had to offer. To Elaine, Rich was her valued husband, not just one more unemployed man.

9. **Affectionate touch.** A gentle and affectionate touch says more than any love song or wonderful poem could ever express. Here we must keep in mind a distinction between

foreplay (which sets in motion a sexual encounter) and affection (which is an end in itself). The kiss of affection is an expression of love and approval, not of desire. With Rich and Elaine, it was hand-holding while strolling through the mall. For you it may be a back rub, a warm hug, a kiss on the cheek, a head on the lap, or a serious case of cuddling.

10. The freedom to laugh lightheartedy at the amusing things that happen in an intimate relationship. Where would any of us be without a good hearty laugh once in a while! While writing this chapter and contemplating these ten factors for achieving intimacy, we were both aware that memories of hilarious and ridiculous moments in our own marriages have brought a good dose of laughter and bonding. Some of the most amusing moments in marriage are some of the most endearing and unforgettable. At times we laugh at ourselves; sometimes we can laugh at the funny things that our mates do. Where there is intimacy and acceptance, laughter is sure to be in abundance. Intimate couples have fun with each other!

Intimacy can be profound and lasting. Think of your fondest memories of times shared with those you cherish most. Was it a walk on the beach? Were there long wordless moments surrounding your closeness? Was it a mingling of words as you enjoyed a picturesque environment together? Sometimes intimacy occurs over the delight of a song or a sunset. Or it can be a deep moment of sharing about a loss, a death or some other pain. Intimacy can be ignited simply by a glance or a touch of the hand. There's a giving and a receiving, an ebb and a flow. Often, conversation is not only a disclosure to another but a disclosure to yourself! For you, the deepest moments of intimacy may arise out of silent conversation, that is, the exchange of a knowing look which speaks, listens, and understands.

Intimacy frees you to be yourself. Intimacy is founded on acceptance. Disclosure of thoughts and feelings and imagination can flow without concern about criticism or judgment. In the safety of intimacy, words flow freely from the heart; there is confidence that the heart, not just the words, will be heard. A deep feeling of acceptance is wrapped around the relationship, allowing the full spectrum of life's emotions—blessings, pain, and grief—to be shared.

WHAT HAVE YOU DONE FOR ME LATELY?

Intimacy is vulnerable to predators. Gary tells this next story of Donna and Kyle, two people working overtime to kill any chance they might have had of finding marital intimacy.

The acrid odor of stalemate permeated the office during Donna and Kyle's entire visit. This couple had previously met with other counselors, some of whom I knew and greatly respected. Why hadn't they been helped? There are usually several possible reasons. Perhaps neither Donna nor Kyle were really willing to negotiate a treaty. Oh, they may have appeared to be willing when they were with the counselor, but apparently they would drop the plan on the way out the door. Perhaps they received a perverse pleasure out of mediated adversity, using the counselor's office for a courtroom and the counselor as a judge or jury. Or, perhaps they didn't trust authority figures and wanted to prove them wrong and incompetent.

It soon became clear that this was one of the more difficult cases I had ever worked with. Kyle was so in love with himself, it was hard to imagine that he really wanted or needed love from Donna. Donna, on the other hand, was in love with her role of being Kyle's victim. Her conversations with friends and relatives were dominated by her complaints of Kyle's latest offenses. When people reached out to comfort her and agree that she had been wronged, Donna was affirmed and rewarded in her role.

One evening as we met together, Kyle asked, "Is it wrong for a man to expect a normal level of sexual activity in a marriage relationship?"

I responded not only to the content of the question, but to its spirit. "Kyle, I support normal sexual activity in marriage wholeheartedly. But I need to ask you something. Do you believe in normal and healthy foreplay before entering into intimate sexual activity with your partner? If I were to ask Donna, I wonder what she would tell me. In fact, I will ask Donna to describe to me your approach to her as her lover and husband."

Donna eagerly answered, "I'm glad you asked! I would love to have a normal sexual relationship with Kyle. But he doesn't have a clue about foreplay. Two weeks ago, he came upstairs and I was almost asleep. It was 12:30 A.M. and Kyle had just finished laughing his way through the David Letterman show. He came to my side of the bed, took off his T-shirt, dropped his pajamas, and said, 'Hey, Donna, how about a little roll in the hay!' And then he belched! I tried to explain to him that I was exhausted and that 12:30 was not a good time to initiate lovemaking! He angrily pulled up his pajamas and marched heavily downstairs, where he proceeded to sleep on the sofa. Frankly, I slept better without him because he snores so loudly. It turned out to be a favor, not a punishment!"

Kyle erupted like Vesuvius, "Take a look at you, Donna! You've gained seventy pounds since we got married. You're just lucky I still want to sleep with you at all!"

Kyle went on, totally unable to restrain himself: "You never think about *my* needs! I do everything to keep food on the table and what do I get in return? There are lots of other tin cans in the dump. And sometimes, I wish I had tried my luck with another one! What do you ever do for me to make me want to come on like some moonstruck lover? There never is a good time with you—at 12:30 or any other time. Why don't you tell the counselor *that!*"

Donna was ten times more subtle than Kyle when delivering her barbs. As tears formed in her eyes, she said with a halting voice, "I think you can see what I have to put up with at home. It's been like this for fourteen years. And if the truth were known, I have often wished that he had chosen another 'tin can,' as he put it, because living with him certainly feels like living in the dump!"

Kyle and Donna had perfected the art of growing apart. They were masters of offending, distancing, and re-offending each other, thus maintaining constant and predictable chaos. Both greatly feared intimacy, yet stayed together because they feared loneliness even more. While there was no biblical reason for it, they divorced. It was simply the by-product of selfishness.

THE TOP TEN PREDATORS OF INTIMACY

What are the predators of intimacy that you need to guard against?

1. **Giving nothing by the basketload.** A partner who gives nothing to the other partner kills the marriage relationship for both. In relation to intimacy, the following statement rings all too true: "You get out of it what you put into it." As many weeks as I spent with Donna and Kyle, I never heard either partner acknowledge that the other had contributed one positive thing to the relationship!

2. **Blame.** There is a dangerous assumption that fixing blame on another will solve a problem. On the contrary, only personal responsibility leads to harmonious solutions to problems. Donna and Kyle were masters of blaming. Solutions remain out of reach for those who build a wall of blame.

Norm Wright, the acclaimed marriage counselor, astutely stated at a marriage seminar, "Most divorces do not end with two angry people. What we find is two exhausted people lying at the base of a wall of indifference which has been built over a long period of time." Our experience as counselors stands in affirmation of this wise insight.

3. **Breaking confidences and gaining advocates outside the relationship.** Nothing disrupts intimacy like an unwanted third party! In their own masterful way, Donna and Kyle sought to misuse their counselor, making him an inappropriate third party, using him to gain an advantage over the other rather than to help them resolve their problems. In many cases, the unwanted third parties are a couple's own children, in-laws, close friends, and at times, perfect strangers. In marriage, two is company, three's a crowd. (A chosen counselor is usually an advocate for the couple, not just one of the partners. Counselors are normally able to avoid being caught in a masterful manipulation, remaining free to instruct or guide the couple toward reasonable solutions.) Whenever a partner confides in a third party who is *unwelcomed* by the mate, the subsequent broken confidences serve to destroy the emotional safety in the relationship, leading to a generalized loss of security between the partners.

4. **Lack of consideration of needs, plans, or preferences.** In an act of selfishness, the needs of the other are deferred or ignored. This selfish lack of consideration is an eloquent expression of the lack of value the partner holds in the eyes of the mate. Kyle's insensitivity to intrude on Donna to meet his own primal sexual needs, when she was exhausted from her day and almost asleep, would have been a crushing blow to any self-respecting partner. Not only did he disregard her condition, he ignored many of the factors

essential for achieving intimate relationships. There was a lack of emotional connection, inconsiderate timing, and a selfish orientation—an instant recipe for hurt and anger.

5. **Critical or demeaning words.** Once you say it, you can't retrieve it, no matter how much you wish you could! It is not likely that either Donna or Kyle will soon forget what the other said in front of a witness during their counseling session. Though it's now years later, the *counselor* can't forget them!

6. **Misplaced anger.** Too often we find it true that "we always hurt the one we love." It is not appropriate to take frustrations and anger out on your partner or your kids when it has nothing to do with them. Sometimes such anger was generated long ago, through events occurring before the couple ever met. There is a place for that anger—but it is not on the head of the innocent. Kyle and Donna may each have feared intimacy due to earlier relationship experiences like an abusive or neglect-laden childhood, or an abusive dating partner. The misplaced anger kept them from getting close, but they never got to the bottom of their problems because they were clouding the issues.

7. **Untimely complaint or correction.** This involves a lack of sensitivity. It also involves changing your role from partner to critical parent, boss, or dictator. The end result will be humiliation and perhaps retaliation. As Christians, we have received instruction regarding the timeliness of a correction, our choice of words, and the importance of maintaining a kind attitude, with an emphasis on the needs of the other person. *Untimely* would include times when our partner is exhausted or ill, when friends or family are present, in front of children, while at work, or whenever or

wherever it would serve to disrupt or hurt. Love shows sensitivity and cares about the feelings of the other.

8. **Never saying you're sorry; never repenting.** Another predator of intimacy is a lack of humility. Humility is necessary to say you're sorry and to change your offending behavior. In three months of counseling, Gary never heard Kyle or Donna apologize for their inappropriate or hurtful behavior.

9. **Lack of empathy.** When one partner learns that the other is in pain, a supportive response is called for, no matter what the source of the pain. Donna had tears in her eyes on several occasions in counseling sessions. It was always Kyle's practice to either stare straight ahead or actually turn his chair away from Donna. There was never an attempt to console, show understanding, or acknowledge the pain. In fact, Kyle held her pain in contempt. This is a deadly practice, a definite predator of intimacy.

10. **Silence.** The predator of silence is not at all like the comfortable quiet of intimacy. This silence haunts and assaults, insults, and demeans, and controls its target. It is the silence of anger. Without any words, it shouts, "I don't care!" choking the life out of intimacy.

GOOD RELATIONSHIPS TAKE LOTS OF QUALITY TIME

Ray Bradbury, the well-known science fiction author, often said it was necessary to write a lot of pages in order to obtain one page of excellence. In contrast is the myth that *quality* time is sufficient where *quantity* time is not available. Experience has shown us that accumulating resentment often builds when one partner neglects spending enough time with the mate to allow the relationship to flourish. Certainly that communicates to the neglected partner that he or she is not a priority. It is unrealistic to expect a neglected partner to respond enthusiastically—when the schedule permits! The truth is that in relationships, as in writing, many hours are required to obtain some precious hours of intimacy. When a relationship receives a great deal of attention and energy, the return on the investment is immensely profitable.

EIGHT

∾

Keeping Romance Alive

Trent and Julia celebrated their first anniversary by spending the weekend at a bed-and-breakfast. They spent two nights in an elegant suite overlooking a rustic mill house. A spiral staircase led from the lobby up to their cozy room. The room captured the spirit of days gone by, blended with all the comforts and beautiful amenities you would hope to find in a Victorian manor.

Julia gasped with delight when they entered their room. She was captured by the romantic glow of the fireplace, thoughtfully prepared in expectation of their arrival. On the cedar chest at the foot of their bed was a lavish bouquet of two dozen roses amid a cloud of baby's breath. Tears filled her eyes as she fell into Trent's arms. She whispered, "You really love me, don't you!" as she kissed him passionately for his thoughtfulness. Trent was filled with the joy of knowing that his love had grown stronger during their first year of marriage. Nothing gave him more pleasure than to see her eyes light up with the joy of being loved.

Julia had purchased a surprise of her own for Trent. She knew he would enjoy her surprise every bit as much as she enjoyed the bouquet! The reservations for dinner pushed them to dress quickly, and then they found themselves amid the irresistible aromas. They were seated in a private booth, and looked at each other through the glow of a single candle, signifying their first anniversary. Trent had taken the time to write Julia a love letter, expressing his deepening feelings of love and gratitude for her.

He held her hand as he read the letter. Her heart melted as she listened to the loving words he had penned and soft tones he spoke. When he was finished, she reached into her purse and presented Trent with a small rectangular box which held two tickets. Trent loved ice hockey, but had never been to an arena for a live game. It had taken Julia a long time, but she managed to save the money and secure front row seats for Trent and his good friend Taylor. Trent couldn't have been more excited. He was delighted with the gift and her willingness to let him share that moment with his best friend. She really knew how to surprise him!

Trent was pretty good at surprises himself. He had overheard Julia talking to her best friend, Tricia, who had just returned from a weekend at a bed-and-breakfast and raved about it. He overheard Julia express a desire to spend a weekend with him there someday. That was all Trent needed. He wrote down the name of the hotel on the back of one of his business cards and made the reservation six months in advance, to be sure he could secure the anniversary date. He even inquired about what they felt was the best room for a young couple celebrating their first anniversary. He was thrilled at their choice.

After dinner, Trent took Julia to a theater a few blocks away from the hotel. He had discovered that *Love Affair* was playing, and hoped it would provide the prelude for their return to the hotel. Boy, did it! Hand in hand they watched scene after enchanting scene, and were charmed by the ending. It was an outstandingly romantic movie, as was the evening.

When they reentered their room, they were greeted with chilled sparkling cider, two crystal goblets, and an array of tasty pastries. Julia had set this surprise in motion earlier, under the pretense of going to the powder room during dinner. Julia looked into Trent's eyes and said, "My dear, you will need to excuse me. I'm going to change into something more comfortable."

Smiling, Trent responded, "I can hardly wait!"

This memorable first anniversary was followed by a steady stream of romantic surprises throughout their marriage. Each delighted as much in the planning as in finding themselves enthralled in the "sweet conspiracies" that continually re-ignited their romance.

Trent had promised Julia that something very special would occur on their tenth anniversary. And, boy, did he come through! They left LAX at 8:00 A.M. on Hawaiian Airlines, arriving five hours and twenty-eight minutes later in Honolulu. Around 4:30 P.M. Honolulu time, they took a shuttle to an adjacent airport and boarded a prop jet to the garden island of Kauai. That evening, after settling in their room, they dined in an elegant marble court amid lush tropical plants and tiki torches. One of the grandest memories of that week in Kauai was enjoying the exquisite sunset from the west-facing balcony of their room.

Their internal clocks told them it was three hours earlier. They were far too awake to settle into their room, so they decided to take a long stroll along the lengthy beachfront near their hotel. The surf caressed the shore while strains of Hawaiian music softly filled the air. The moon created a splash of diamonds over the bay. Julia had never felt more in love, as she was cradled in the cleft of Trent's shoulder and protective arm.

Trent had saved for three years for this romantic getaway, all the while gathering tidbits of information about the island of Kauai. Now in Hawaii, they found even the days to be romantic. They didn't know a single person on the island, but it didn't matter. Romance is a one-on-one arrangement. Finding things to say had never been a problem for Trent and Julia. Talking was especially free-flowing here, where so much color and beauty surrounded them. Wild orchids were to be found all over, with hibiscus-lined driveways and walkways of fallen blossoms. The trade winds brought an intoxicating potpourri of fragrances.

Julia and Trent had truly discovered paradise—everything they had hoped they'd find and more. The food was abundant and exotically flavorful; the people friendly, giving the impression that their sole purpose in life was to serve Julia and Trent. They felt like royalty.

By the end of the week, they could hardly believe the many experiences they had enjoyed. The activities were relaxing, the people were mellow, and the atmosphere was hypnotic. The greatest gift of the week was the ability to place the garden of their relationship into a paradise of God's making.

A million people could go to Hawaii and not enjoy the pleasures that Julia and Trent tasted. What was unique about Julia and Trent was the essence they took with them to the island. For ten years they had nurtured the romance between them. Their romance had matured into a practiced art. They were very married.

The goal of a lover is to become one with the beloved. That's why lovers are pictured face-to-face and friends are pictured side by side. So says C.S. Lewis in *The Four Loves*. He explains these four loves as *agape* (perfect, unconditional love), *storge* (affection), *eros* (romance), and *philos* (friendship). He says eros love entails a unique desire to be alone with the beloved, while the other three loves flourish in groups and may even be enhanced by a greater number of people.

In other words, romance flourishes one on one. "Two's company, three's a crowd." With nonromantic love relationships, on the other hand, "the more the merrier."

By cultivating romance in your marriage, you will contribute to the depth, the longevity, the quality, and the pleasure of the greatest human connection you will ever have!

SO, WHAT'S THE FORMULA?

So how do you get there from here? How do you keep the romance in your marriage, or revive it if it has died?

1. Say it with flowers. Recently, in a church course on marriage, Gary asked the women in the group what they considered romantic. One woman shyly raised her hand and said, "I like flowers!" Gary kidded the ladies by giving the male point of view, that giving flowers is difficult because flowers had become expensive and it was hard to watch your investment in a relationship wilt before your eyes!

The shy contributor said, "Maybe it would be helpful for you to know why women like flowers. First of all, since we were little girls, we have watched Miss Americas and Rose Queens and Miss Universes being handed bouquets of flowers. So, it makes us feel special when we receive them. Secondly, and probably most importantly, there is only one reason you would give flowers, and that reason is to say, 'I love you!'"

Well, folks, there you have it!

2. Go away alone for the weekend. We recommend that you plan weekend retreats once per quarter, minimum. If finances are an obstacle, go away for the day. The operative word here is *alone*. No children, no friends, no parents, just you two. This time together is a reenactment of your honeymoon. Something special usually happens in beautiful settings, lingering over well-prepared meals, and staying in beautifully appointed rooms away from all responsibilities. You focus only on each other and let the rest of the world become a fog.

3. Express your love often. Say "I love you," and follow it with your beloved's name. Embrace often. Send admiring glances. Offer gentle touches along with soft words that tell your partner how much you love being together.

4. **Date your mate.** It is important to your marriage that the courtship never end. Keep doing the very thing that developed the relationship in the first place. Dating allows for interesting activities, time alone and the making of fun memories. There is adventure and surprise ahead, planned just by you. By the way, if you haven't tried it, alternate the planning. Women plan great dates. Men do, also. Plan dates around your favorite personal interests, your mutual tastes, and even surprise your mate with a plan to do his or her favorite thing.

5. **Mark your calendar in advance showing special events.** Plan ahead for your mate's birthday, your anniversary, and other holidays and special events. The idea is to keep things special, not as second thoughts. Make reservations for dinner or accommodations in advance. It shows you are anticipating the event with enthusiasm. You may even wish to leave hints that will tantalize your mate's imagination. For example, a business card from a travel agent left on the dresser would serve this purpose. Or, shopping for a dress or shirt and tie for your mate and not telling them why. There are ways to say, "I'm thinking of you!" that are unmistakable. That is part of the romance.

6. **Love notes and thought cards never go out of style.** There is something so tangible and real about love written in your mate's handwriting! Receiving a note that tells you you're loved and why, is one of life's greatest joys. If you are not a writer, find a card which portrays your feelings and add your own touch with a few lines of your own. This will delight your partner every time. Again and again.

7. Romance thrives in beautiful settings. Seen a sunset lately? The light of the sunset's colorful reflection sparkling across an ocean or lake, or simply lighting the face of your beloved, is a sight to behold often. A corner booth in a quaint restaurant shared by the two of you, with only the light of a flickering candle, emanates the same intimate warmth. Holding hands in a dim movie theater while you enjoy a love story on the screen may evoke memories of your own romantic journey. Closer to home, fresh linens on the bed, a soft spray of perfume or cologne, soft music—and two well-groomed partners—are inviting features to enhance marital romance. There are many ways to enhance the immediate environment to nurture romance. There are any number of favorite settings you share with your mate. If this is new to you, explore together and create your own special memories.

Discuss these ideas with your partner. You may have some questions about what your mate has enjoyed the most in the past. You may each have some personal wishes that you would like to fulfill in romancing your marriage. Write down some of the ideas you discuss and tuck them away for future reference. Romance is a mixture of quality and quantity time, designed just for two. Enjoy!

NINE

Growing Together: Managing Differences

We would like to introduce you to three couples, each having one thing in common: a wide range of individual differences. What's also different is their methods of managing those differences. Differences can be viewed as either assets or liabilities. Where one may perceive the differences as tearing the couple apart, another may perceive them as an enhancement that creates a healthy diversity. These couples illustrate three distinct models for managing differences.

INTERPERSONAL RELATIONSHIP

Doyle and Joyce offer a good example of living in an interpersonal relationship. Their interaction exemplifies the type of relationship most couples long for.

Doyle sat quietly in the back corner of a booth at Millie's, his favorite coffee shop. He routinely spent one hour a day nursing a cup of coffee and consuming one order of dry wheat toast before he rushed off to Oakborough High School to teach American Literature. He was intensely familiar with the classics, ranging from John Steinbeck to Mark Twain. So voracious was his appetite for reading that it would be hard to suggest someone familiar whose works he hadn't read. Tom Clancy, John Grisham, James Michener, Stephen King, Ray Bradbury, and Michael Crichton had become his literary friends. He had spent countless hours analyzing their work so that he might explain it with a sense of wonder to his enthusiastic and grateful students.

For months now he had been experiencing a restlessness that he had slowly become able to define. He realized that he and his wife, Joyce, were no longer the same two people who naively and optimistically joined hands in marriage over a decade ago. Doyle had reviewed the last thirteen years and could plainly see that he was the one who had changed.

He remembered clearly adoring Joyce because of her soft and gentle and nonconfrontational style of conversation. He realized now that he preferred a stirring discussion that romped through political and philosophical concepts. His favorite pastimes had become attending heady plays, thought-provoking films, stimulating discussions, golf, hiking, and carpentry.

These interests had evolved slowly. He recalled that at age twenty-two, when he met Joyce, the biggest question they faced as a couple was whether or not to go to a college party. They were both "social," and for the most part their friends were not into the deeper issues of life: They were well matched.

Having graduated from college, Doyle enjoyed the light and airy freedom to personally choose how he would develop intellectually. Over the years, Doyle's intellectual pursuits enabled him to contribute something of substance to almost every conversation he encountered. It was satisfying and stimulating, and his habit of learning only increased as the years passed.

Joyce was proud of her husband's knowledge, often deferring to him for information or the answer to questions posed in a social setting. She, however, sought family-oriented pursuits to fulfill her life. She was mother to three, and devoted herself to that role. Her reading focused on children's books and parenting books. She rarely read an entire book. Her daily contacts consisted of her children's playmates, other mothers, girlfriends, her children's teachers, and neighbors.

Make no mistake about it: Joyce was a very capable and intelligent woman. Her incredible management of her household qualified her as a CEO. Her shrewd judgment of human behavior led to sound and wise responses to the practical issues she faced on a daily basis. She intuitively knew what to say to encourage her children and inspire them to do their best in school. She was able to love her children in such a way that none was jealous of the other. She had a large collection of close friends. She chose them wisely. She was an outstanding leader and team player. Joyce was flourishing in her chosen niche.

Doyle finished his cup of coffee, sliding the saucer to the end of the table to have it refilled. The coffee shop was his private retreat. He was able to affirm Joyce's skills as a mother. But he felt other gnawing feelings. He felt that a chasm had formed and separated them. He felt guilty, because he knew that he had built the chasm. Yet he didn't think it was appropriate to feel guilty, because his acquisition of knowledge had been a good thing, not a bad thing.

He recalled that when he and Joyce had attended a party during the Gulf War, someone had mentioned Norman Schwarzkopf. Joyce remarked, "Who's that?" and an enormous wave of laughter filled the room. Her friends thought she was kidding, but she was not. Doyle felt embarrassed, even though he realized that everyone thought she was kidding. He also remembered an occasion when Joyce was asked a question about her opinion of Rose Bird (the controversial California Supreme Court Justice). Joyce wistfully commented, "Oh, she must be a nice lady. She's the one who frees all the wildlife!" Again, others' laughter camouflaged her lack of political awareness. Her best friend said, "Joyce, what a kidder you are!" and Joyce just smiled. One of Joyce's best qualities was her sense of security. She liked who she was, and experienced no shame when her limitations were exposed.

In remembering those incidents, Doyle again experienced

that gnawing feeling, a feeling that told him something was missing. He thought maybe all he needed was a vacation. Then he stopped. Giving it more thought, he realized that he had a problem and couldn't run from it, but it was his problem, not hers. He was the one who was uncomfortable, not Joyce. He was the one who felt embarrassed, not Joyce. His value judgments had been fueled by his false expectations. He had imposed his own list of goals on his wife, expecting her to match him in his intellectual pursuits. Those imposed expectations would never be fulfilled and he knew it. She was not even aware that he had those expectations. Further, if she did know, she would say, "You want me to be someone I am not, nor want to be."

Doyle realized once again that Joyce's and his commitment to each other was the most important thing in his life. So what was he going to do to relieve this gnawing feeling? He began to question the unrealistic expectations he had projected onto his wife. He decided to recognize her interests and strengths as being separate from his own. He came to grips with the fact that he had to change. He could be satisfied with his chosen intellectual pursuits and it was up to him to create the outlets for that satisfaction.

He decided to take definitive action. First, he set out to find a close male friend who shared his intellectual interests. He determined to spend some significant time cultivating a friendship with that person. He knew himself well enough to know that choosing a female companion for deep discussion meant opening himself up to the possibility of a romantic involvement that would destroy his marriage.

Second, he adjusted his perspective to appreciate and affirm Joyce just as she was, not as he had fantasized her to be. In his heart, Doyle knew there wasn't one other woman on the earth that he would want for a life partner and to be the mother of his children. She was the most wonderful friend he had ever had. With delight, he thought about how much their children were already reflecting the fine qualities he cherished so much in Joyce. Who was he to change the rules midstream, just because some of his interests had changed. Nobody had died and made him God! He now realized he had been acting like a petty dictator in Joyce's life, projecting his expectations and demands on her. What an eye-opening realization! As he reasoned this out, the empty space he had felt deep within was dissipating.

Doyle made an inner change that day. He made a promise to himself to demonstrate appreciation and notice Joyce's many contributions, and to speak his love to her often. This decision marked a turning point in their marriage—a turning point toward growth and intimacy. He discussed his internal conflict with Joyce. He reassured her that the struggle was his own, and he had come to terms with himself and the expectations he was imposing on Joyce. Their relationship began to flourish all the more. Discussion and understanding increased their sense of mutual respect. They accommodated and celebrated their differences, negotiating room for each of them to be themselves.

Doyle and Joyce's relationship developed into what we call an *interpersonal* relationship, which has the following characteristics:

- Open expression of each other's expectations
- High value to individual thoughts, feelings, preferences
- High communication and negotiation
- Emotional climate of acceptance
- High desire to resolve conflict
- Shared experiences seen as enhancing the individual partner
- Individual experiences seen as enhancing the relationship
- Differences appreciated, accommodated, celebrated

Keep this list in mind as a model for how you want your relationships to work. Read each item on the list and ask yourself if you and your spouse are practicing these fine elements of the interpersonal relationship. No couple exercises all of those elements all of the time. The degree to which you practice the principles of an interpersonal relationship will have a direct bearing on the degree of joy and fulfillment experienced in the marriage. Differences can be accommodated within an interpersonal relationship in such a way as to bring satisfaction to both partners.

COEXISTENT RELATIONSHIP

We now introduce you to Sandy and Roger. They offer a good example of living in a coexistent relationship. Their interaction exemplifies the type of relationship that leads to deep loneliness. For some, the marriage lasts a lifetime. For others, the marraige ends in divorce.

Sandy awakened and looked across the bed, but Roger was gone. She resented his predictability, though early on in the marriage she would have listed predictability as one of Roger's strong points. Roger was a hardworking plumber, and left the home every morning just before 5 A.M. Sandy couldn't remember Roger missing a day of work for any reason. She had come to resent him even for that. She went downstairs to make coffee, eat breakfast, and read the newspaper. She didn't have to be at the beauty salon until nine o'clock.

As exciting as her salon business had become, it still wasn't enough. She wanted more and could have looked for it in the wrong places, but she had made promises. On more than one occasion, she reviewed the promises and searched through the Bible looking for loopholes for leaving a marriage. Finding none that applied to her, she found herself praying for Roger to have an affair so that she might have an honorable reason for leaving. But he was loyal as a collie, though considerably more boring.

When she wasn't working at the salon, Sandy was at the stable riding, jumping, and grooming her horse, Jubilant. The affection she received from the horse was ten times more satisfying than anything she was given by her husband. One of the things she resented most was that Roger never resented the inordinate amount of time she was spending with the horse. Once she asked, "Doesn't it bother you that I spend so much time at the stable?" He just remarked that it gave him more time to spend in the garage, where one project after another beckoned him.

Sandy had found herself growing increasingly irritable, but could not even provoke Roger into an argument. He always deferred to her, saying that if she was happy, he was happy. She realized, suddenly, that the reason they had no conflicts was because they had no relationship. Something clarified in her mind: How stupid I was five years ago to brag to my friends that we had no conflicts in our marriage. The truth is, we had no conflicts because we had no relationship!

Roger didn't visit Sandy's jumping competitions, and she couldn't remember the last time she had set foot in the garage. Sandy cared nothing about the sights and sounds of Roger's plumbing projects, and Roger couldn't understand why anyone would want to sit on the back of a nine-hundred-pound animal that occasionally jumped over a pile of stubble or a plank.

Sandy took a sip of coffee while she stared at the sagging and frayed cushion on the couch, from which Roger viewed hundreds of thousands of hours worth of television. His lack of discernment in what he watched never ceased to amaze her. There were only so many times that Sandy could watch "Brady Bunch" reruns and remain focused. For Roger, it was always a thrill to see the program resolve in such a happy and predictable way.

Roger had never been a sexual dynamo, but as the years had passed, he seemed to show absolutely no interest in sexual activity. Sandy felt mixed emotions about this. On the one hand, it would have been nice to be desired, but on the other hand there was a certain relief that she would not have to entertain someone who enjoyed so little of her respect.

Sandy just plain resented her marriage. She and Roger had so little in common. They had separate friends, separate careers, separate schedules, separate recreations—and for the last three years, separate beds. Roger's immediate assent to that request was perhaps the most demeaning; he had simply said, "That'll be fine. You'll probably sleep better."

Sandy was at a dangerous point as she entertained a very dangerous thought. "Whatever God would do to me for leaving Roger couldn't be worse than living with him." Two weeks later, she filed for a divorce.

Following aresome characteristics of the *coexistent* relationship:

- Rigid boundaries
- Low valuing of each individual
- Low communication and negotiation
- Closed, cold emotional climate
- Low desire to resolve conflict
- Few shared experiences
- Individual experiences reign
- Differences criticized, grudgingly tolerated, or allowed to create conflict

Review the above list and see if you can identify these characteristics in Sandy and Roger's relationship. If you see any of these in your own relationship, refer to the list of characteristics of the interpersonal relationship for a model to guide your changes. For example, low communication and low negotiation in the coexistent relationship is replaced by high communication and high negotiation; the closed, cold emotional climate is replaced by a climate of acceptance.

ENMESHED RELATIONSHIP

We now introduce you to Rodney and Violet, who have an "enmeshed" relationship. On the surface, it appears to be a healthy arrangement for both partners. But you will see that, along with some compatibility and fulfillment, there is a stifling of growth, and dissatisfaction.

It was New Year's Day and Rodney and Violet were playing the roles they had played for twenty-seven years. As the snow fell gently on the hills of Ann Arbor, Michigan, Violet was making the final preparations for the exquisite New Year's dinner that kicked off every year in the Clark family. Rodney, on the other hand, was preparing to watch a myriad of bowl games, from the Cotton Bowl to the grandaddy of them all, the Rose Bowl. USC was pitted against the University of Michigan and Rodney was a Wolverine, tried and true. The University of Michigan was Rodney's alma mater, the school that taught him electrical engineering. Not only was he going to celebrate his twenty-eighth wedding anniversary in June, but he would also be experiencing his twenty-eighth anniversary of employment with General Motors in Detroit.

Rodney's daughter and three sons began to arrive, and they and each of their mates took a different turn as they entered the warm confines of the Clark home. The women all found their way to the large kitchen, settled on stools around the cooking island, and busied themselves with chatter and snack preparation for game time. Rodney bellowed out a gregarious, "You guys get in here! They're just about to kick off!" Rodney had a self-satisfied smile because he had just purchased a big-screen television. In no time, the family room was alive with the primal cheers of the male members of the Clark clan, while the female members quietly caught each other up on the latest achievements of their children.

Rodney bellowed out, "Violet, when are we gonna get some snacks in here? All these breadwinners are starvin'!"

Momentarily, a spread of food appeared that covered the surface of their large coffee table, even the end table.

Lucy, Violet's daughter, asked, "When's Dad going to buy you some new carpet, Mom?" Violet smiled and said, "That would be nice, honey. But there's a few more years left in this one. Maybe when your father gets through finishing his workshop, he'll consider a new carpet. He doesn't think we need one right now." Lucy just nodded, acquiescing to what she believed was a man's right to make important decisions in his home. She remembered her father preparing her mother to vote correctly when she went to the polls in November. They never argued, and her mother constantly asked for permission: to buy a dress, call a friend, participate in a social function; she even asked for guidance in what the children would be permitted to do. She had no really close friends or anything that could be identified as independent or individual pursuits. She existed to serve Rodney. If he was home, he insisted that she be there also. Even when he was away, Violet only left the house to obtain things or run errands that made his life run smoothly. The truth was, Rodney couldn't even brew a pot of coffee without Violet. He would be lost if he were to lose her. Who would match his socks to his outfit, who would pack his lunch or choose his tie?

In social settings Violet was an ornament. In any lively conversation, she was there to be seen and not heard, to speak only to affirm the lofty thoughts of others. Rodney was not always careful about how he spoke of her, and was a little too free to discredit her intellectual capabilities. This hurt Violet, but she was a very positive woman and wrote it off. "That's just the way Rodney is...," she'd say, not taking it so personally that her emotions spilled over into anger or hatred. As the years passed, she didn't really notice the things that were being lost to her: the classes she never took, the friends she never made, the outings she only dreamed about, the places she visited only in the pages of magazines and periodicals. Rodney went on hunting trips with the guys at work, but she was not even permitted to go to the women's retreat at church. When she simply asked to go to lunch with a girlfriend, Rodney would scornfully say, "It'd be cheaper if she came over here!"

This afternoon, like so many, ended when all of the china and crystal was returned to the places they had occupied for twenty-seven years, when the carpet was vacuumed, and when the last bowl game was reviewed by the announcers and the most valuable player had received his award. After the family left, Violet walked upstairs and laid Rodney's pajamas neatly on the end of the bed, turned back the covers, and fluffed his pillow.

Two months later, she died.

It was not long after the funeral that Rodney and all the children realized how much they had taken Violet for granted. But none were as lost as Rodney. He was truly beside himself. He felt as though he didn't know how to put one foot in front of the other. It was his sense of helplessness that drove him to a widows and widowers group. In the group he found a woman who seemed to be as lost as he was. And despite advice from friends that he should take his time to experience the grief process before entertaining a new relationship, he sought this woman's companionship. Much to the offense of his children, he began dating her only two months after Violet's memorial service. He was remarried in six months to a woman who took up where Violet had left off.

Following are some characteristics of an *enmeshed* relationship:

- Blurred boundaries
- Overdependency on each other
- Demanding and controlling communication
- Extremes in emotional climate—either suffocating or abandoning

- False, temporary conflict resolution
- Extreme involvement and possessiveness
- Individual experiences viewed as threats to the relationship
- Differences viewed as a challenge to remold and build compliance in the partner

If you and your spouse are involved in an enmeshed marital relationship, you will be experiencing many of these characteristics. Again, note the items on the list that are true in your relationship, and then compare those same items to the characteristics of the interpersonal relationship. Notice that, in the enmeshed relationship, differences are viewed as a challenge to remold and build compliance into (control) the partner, whereas in the interpersonal relationship, differences are appreciated, accommodated, and even celebrated.

CHECK YOUR RELATIONSHIP STYLE

Now that you have gained a clearer understanding of the three most common ways of dealing with differences in the marriage relationship, we encourage you to use the following exercises to determine the style of relationship you have with your mate: interpersonal, coexistent, or enmeshed. We have created several different scenarios and three responses to each. Read the scenario and then circle the response that you feel most typifies how you would respond. Circle the letter *I*, *C*, or *E*, according to the response you would most likely make as a couple:

1. *There is an upcoming awards banquet at the husband's place of employment. He may be up for an award.*

   I: After a discussion, you determine that it would be politically incorrect not to support the function, though both of you, especially the wife, would rather be anywhere but the banquet. You make it a positive experience by enjoying each other.

C: The husband attends the banquet, and the wife goes out with her girlfriends. He had never expected her to attend. She wouldn't have even if asked.

E: The only thing undecided is what the husband will tell his wife to wear. She sees it as her role to make her husband look good. So, they both attend.

2. *You are attending an extended family gathering at Thanksgiving. Which of these descriptions best fits you as a couple?*

I: You spend a good deal of time interacting with family members, sitting next to each other as a couple. Separately, you also take individual time with family members who are especially dear to you. After the gathering you share interesting and pertinent information about your visits, as well as your current feelings about the family.

C: From the moment of arrival until the time of departure, you talk with whomever you wish. You are not found together at the gathering except at the assigned seating and the silent drive home. Once home, rarely do you share anything about the visit.

E: You are together constantly, experiencing the same encounters. One of you depends on the other to carry the conversation and interpret the information you gather.

3. *It's a Saturday afternoon. Both of you have had busy weeks, with little time to interact.*

I: You discuss what each of you would like to do with the day. You remember whose needs and desires have been most recently gratified. Out of a sense of fairness and consideration, you choose to do something together for part of the day, leaving some time for each to relax around the house.

C: You get up in the morning to find that your mate has already left, and there are no plans to do anything together. This has become a common experience; you rarely know each other's whereabouts on the weekends and do not consider each other when making your plans.

E: The man does traditionally male things like gardening and the woman does housecleaning and shopping. In the afternoon and evening, the dominant member of the family chooses what, if anything, to do, and both do it together.

4. *In planning the summer vacation, which of these scenarios best depicts your method of decision making?*

I: A good deal of time is spent asking your mate, "Where would you most enjoy going? What would you most enjoy including in the activities?" Then, plans are made well in advance that meet many of each mate's hopes and wishes for the vacation. Both partners are excited about their (truly *their*, not his or her) vacation.

C: Your mate announces that he or she has planned a vacation. You are informed about the departure and return dates and times, and left free to do what you would like to do while your mate is gone. There is no discussion about a joint vacation. Or, there is a vacation planned in terms of location, but not activities. You and your mate simply take your uninvolved lifestyle on the road and plant it in another location.

E: One mate tells the other the itinerary for the vacation, including location and activities. There is little discussion. They carefully plan the details and follow through together by participating in their predictable outing.

5. *The question comes up about whether the wife should work outside of the home. Which of these responses would you expect from the husband in your home?*

I: The husband engages in a thorough discussion, helping discover the pros and cons of his wife's working outside the home. His underlying attitude is one of support as he comes to understand her needs. She is not afraid to hear his opinions, because she has come to trust that his only interest is the best interest of their marriage. She will have a good deal of independence to make this decision after they have processed it together.

C: The husband's underlying attitude is expressed well by his detached, "Whatever." He may be glad that his wife is willing to work and finance her own follies. At any rate, he is indifferent to her decision.

E: The dominating husband may insist that his wife work outside the home without reducing her household responsibilities. On the other hand, he may forbid her to work on the basis that his personal needs may be sacrificed on the altar of unnecessary material gain.

6. *As a couple, how do your models of interaction work with your friendships? Choose the example that best describes your style.*

I: We are friends with other couples who enrich our lives, we welcome our mate's friends into our home, and we each have same-gender friends of our own. We enjoy being with our mutual friends, and willingly carve out time for each other to engage in our personal friendships.

C: We rarely have couples in our life with whom we spend time. Most of the time, we develop outside friendships with individuals of both genders and couples, all unknown to our mate. Our social lives do not meet. Our friends do not know each other. The home is rarely used as a center for social activity; it is merely a place to eat.

E: The dominant mate chooses the couples and individuals who visit the home or attend social events with the couple. The subordinate mate's social life is left to chance. If the couples chosen by the dominant mate happen to be a good match, then the subordinate mate may make a good friendship connection. All too often, however, that is not the case.

Now that you have completed this exercise, see which letter you selected most often. If you chose *C*, your relationship is probably coexistent; if you chose *E*, it is probably enmeshed; if you chose *I*, congratulations are in order because your relationship is interpersonal! As we stated earlier, interpersonal relationships offer couples the most opportunity for personal and marital fulfillment.

For those of you who have identified that your relationship is either coexistent or enmeshed, we recommend careful consideration of several chapters in this book. In chapter two, "He Made Them Male and Female," we define marriage as a divine partnership. This chapter offers guidelines for developing a partnership-oriented marriage. That is part of the interpersonal relationship. Further, we suggest you review chapter seven, "A Journey into Deepening Friendship," to learn the heartbeat of intimacy. Chapter eleven, "I'm in Charge Here!" deals with the issues of control, and would help mitigate an enmeshed relationship. In the chapter following, "Keeping In-Laws in Line," you will find help in breaking enmeshed relationships with parents.

If you find you are in a coexistent relationship, we recommend you seek professional help. This type of relationship has resentment at its core, and it would be most productive for you to have some direction for reducing that resentment. It takes a long time to build up the pain necessary to finally develop a coexistent relationship. Of course such a buildup of resentment requires special care and help to unload: Chapter ten, "Arguing for Fun and Profit," is a good place to begin breaking down the pattern that leads to two people avoiding each other.

This book is dedicated to helping you develop an interpersonal relationship in your marriage, under the Ephesians 5 model of partnership. The mutual respect and love portrayed in God's design for marriage offers the fulfillment and joy God wants for all marriage partners.

TEN

∾

Arguing for Fun and Profit: Conflict Resolution

F ew of us enter marriage with good skills for resolving con- flict. We arrive with behaviors that we have observed in our own families or practiced on the playground. All too often, fall- back clichés like, "Sticks and stones can break my bones, but words will never hurt me," "Shut up!," or "Because I said so!" are our most sophisticated debating tools.

It is a given that any two people will approach life in two different ways, and conflict will result. In our opinion, if a cou- ple has no conflict, they have a major problem. Most likely one partner is not represented in the marriage. Occasional conflict is a healthy indication that no one is being robbed of his or her individuality. The hallmark of maturity in your marriage is not whether or not you have conflicts, but how you handle them.

Scripture offers a starting point for handling all of life's con- flicts. We are to begin with a humble spirit:

But the fruit of the Spirit is love, joy, peace, patience, kind- ness, goodness, faithfulness, gentleness, and self-control.... Let us not become conceited, provoking and envying each other. **Galatians 5:22, 26**

An attitude of humility is the single most important tool for conflict resolution. St. Francis of Assisi expressed this attitude eloquently in his celebrated prayer:

Prayer of St. Francis of Assisi

Lord,
Make me an instrument of your peace;
Where there is hatred, let me sow love;
Where there is injury, pardon;
Where there is doubt, faith;
Where there is despair, hope;
Where there is darkness, light;
Where there is sadness, joy.

O Divine Master,
Grant that I may not so much
seek to be consoled as to console,
To be understood as to understand;
To be loved as to love.
For it is in giving that we receive.
It is in pardoning that
we are pardoned.
It is in dying that we
are born to eternal life.

Constructive arguing can remove the distance that has developed between you and your mate. It can help you feel closer to each other again. Fair fighting is healthy, not something to be avoided. Strong negative feelings about each other signify that feelings have been hurt, but you can do something to alleviate the negative feelings and make room for more positive and effective interaction in the future.

Let's look at a model for fair fighting and conflict resolution which combines the best methods we have seen couples use successfully.

GUIDELINES FOR A CONFLICT RESOLUTION SESSION

1. **Maintain a solution-oriented mindset.** The solution is more important than determining who is responsible for the problem. Ask yourself, "How may I contribute to the solution?" instead of, "How can I prove I'm right and you're wrong?" Make a list of possible solutions, realizing there is rarely just one solution to a problem. Freely talk over the merits and problems of each suggested solution, staying focused on issues, not personalities.

2. **Accurately state the problem.** Clearly explain the problem as you see it. Be specific and brief when you talk. Put the issue on the table so that it can be resolved. It may help you to write the problem down and read it back to yourself for clarification. Often, defining a problem is half the solution.

3. **Set a reasonable time and pick a safe and appropriate place for your discussion.** Not too early, not too late, never too hungry, never too tired, never in front of the children, and not in public. Choose a setting comfortable for both partners.

4. **Avoid using extreme terms.** For example, "you always" and "you never." Superlatives provoke a defensive attitude, and leave little room for negotiation.

5. **Use responsible language.** Avoid "you" statements as much as possible. They often serve to accuse or fix blame. Express your position in "I" and "me" terms, such as, "I feel hurt when I don't see you very much. I have not felt that I am high on your priority list. I want to talk about this." "I" statements leave room for discussion and resolution. The focus is on the behavior or problem, not on blaming or accusing. Here are some examples:

Recommended	Not Recommended
I miss you and would like to spend more time with you.	You're never home. You don't care about me.
I would feel more like a partner if we could discuss our purchases together.	You're selfish! You always buy things just for yourself!
I would like you to listen while I complete my comment.	Stop interrupting me! You never listen!
It would help me if you were consistently affectionate with me before suggesting lovemaking.	What do you think I am, a light switch?

6. **Take responsibility for your part.** Before you speak, carefully consider this question: "How might my behavior have contributed to this problem or misunderstanding?" Allow for the possibility that you may have unknowingly participated in the difficulties you are now working through. Perhaps it was you alone who set them in motion. You will grow in maturity and courage as you take responsibility for your part. It seems to be a natural fear that admitting to our own shortcomings will diminish us. Actually, taking responsibility for our own part causes others to respect us more.

7. **Speak the truth in love.** Remember that "a gentle answer turns away wrath, but a harsh word stirs up anger" (Proverbs 15:1). How you say it is as important as, if not more important than, what you say. Avoid sarcasm, name calling, and harsh tones.

8. **Be aware of body language.** Try to avoid provoking body language such as rolling your eyes, smirking, crossing your arms, or shaking your head—not to mention obscene and offensive gestures! A condescending parent-child posture would be less than effective at building a solution. Communications experts agree that more than 80 percent of our communication is nonverbal. That means we read each other far beyond what our words say!

   On the positive side, speaking kindly, and maintaining an attentive and expectant posture and gentle eye contact, are all demonstrations of love which will not go unnoticed.

9. **Listen, without formulating a defense.** Repress your own response as you listen to your mate's feelings. (You will share your response after step ten.)

10. **Summarize to offer feedback.** After you have listened to your mate, summarize what you have heard your partner say, to see if there was understanding between you. Ask your mate to confirm that you have heard him or her correctly. If you have, you may now give your own viewpoint and responses. (Your partner will then offer feedback.)

11. **Participate in the solution.** Clearly define tasks that each person may perform to accomplish a solution, and set up a follow-up procedure to monitor progress.

12. **Be prepared for:**
   - Situations to change slowly
   - Brick walls (perhaps even agree to disagree, at least for now)
   - Compromise, negotiation, and renegotiation
   - Occasionally, repentance and miraculous change
   - Some failures. If you are angry, you may overstate, oversimplify, or overreact to the problem that is confronting you. If the anger persists, or no resolution can be found,

a competent third party of your mutual choice might provide objectivity. (This does not mean, "Hey, let's get my best friend's opinion. He'll agree with me!") Scripture encourages seeking wise counsel. That may be a friend, a pastor, or a professional counselor.

13. When you have come to an agreement:

- Affirm each other for helpful contributions: Be specific in affirming attentive listening, effective suggestions, or an open attitude. Let each other know what made the difference.
- Help each partner feel a sense of completion: Simply state the problem, the solution, and your hopefulness for the future. Ask your partner if he or she feels understood, has had ample opportunity to talk, and feels a sense of completion.

Remember, you are looking for improvement, not perfection. Learn to be satisfied when *most* of your conflicts are resolved! The art of fair fighting and conflict resolution dramatically adds a dimension of security to your marriage. These essential and profitable skills can be learned. It is well worth practicing the guidelines to acquire these skills, in order to preserve and nurture your marriage.

ELEVEN

৵

I'm In Charge Here!

You've heard it said that "when something appears too good to be true, it probably is." Bruce was too good to be true. Patty had not yet seen any sign that he was anything but the pot of gold at the end of the rainbow. They had gone together for four months, and Patty believed she had all the information she needed to say yes when he proposed marriage. Bruce even convinced the veteran counselor that he would make a good companion for Patty.

Bruce and Patty completed a personality test. Bruce's scores showed him to be dominant, but not unreasonably so. On the same test, Patty's scores revealed her to be submissive, but not so extreme as to qualify as a *doormat*. Their counselor emphasized their need to monitor that area of their marriage so that Bruce's strength would not overwhelm Patty's weakness to the point that she would gradually give up her identity and be under his control. During their six weeks of premarital counseling, they discussed the concept of partnership and agreed on its principles.

The counselor had noted a few things that seemed unusual. At times, Bruce would seem to be uncomfortable, shifting from side to side in his chair. The counselor also noted that Bruce always dressed in a shirt and tie, even on days that he didn't go to his office. Lastly, the counselor noted that Bruce was very organized and always prepared for the counseling sessions. His assignments were always computer-generated and printed exquisitely on a laser printer. That was refreshing, but very unlike most of the counselor's male clients, who either failed to do the assignment or brought them on napkins from restaurants visited just before the meeting. The counselor wrote it off as positive, thinking that Patty could benefit from Bruce's contribution of order in her life, since order often evokes a feeling of security in marriage.

The counselor only challenged one thing: Bruce's tendency to change his point of view or "see the light" when he would see that his opinion on a particular issue was not compatible with the point of view expressed by his fiancée or the counselor. As time went on the counselor concluded that Bruce had been showing that he was flexible.

The greatest discomfort between Bruce and Patty was generated over male and female roles. Bruce expressed a desire to "be responsible for the leadership of his home." He then defined that statement in terms of a *male-controlled marriage*, instead of a *God-designed partnership*. When confronted, he again convincingly backed down from his hard-line position. So well-polished was his performance that he fooled the counselor, the partner, and perhaps even himself.

On their first morning home from the honeymoon Bruce left early for work. Patty could only remember that she had turned briefly out of a deep sleep to say good-by, kiss him, and tell him that she loved him. Bruce had gotten up at 4:30 A.M. and had spent some time at his computer, generating a two-page document. The first page had a list of ten things he insisted Patty accomplish that day, and the second half was a short devotional with a Bible verse to memorize. As he had written his piece, he had italicized certain words and phrases he thought applied specifically to Patty. Then he propped the note up in front of a milk carton in the refrigerator.

After Patty awakened, she made her way to the kitchen for breakfast and, opening the refrigerator door, saw the note. Her first thought was, "How sweet. A note from Bruce." Next came dismay as she was rudely introduced to the reality that her husband saw her as a helpless child in need of his superior direction. She would soon discover that Bruce saw her as a slave to his wants and his desires, not as a partner or an equal.

When Bruce came home late that afternoon, Patty expressed her confusion and confronted Bruce about the tone and purpose of the note. Bruce seized this moment as his opportunity to set her straight about some things. (We hope you neither use nor hear this bullying approach in your marriage!) She was told that, regardless of what he had said in the counseling sessions, he had the godly conviction that he was the head of the household and she had better get used to it. Any attempt on her part to express herself was met with his rage and scorn. He belittled her until 2:00 A.M. and then had the nerve to attempt to initiate lovemaking.

Rebuffed, he turned his back to her and quickly fell asleep. She quietly cried herself to sleep. He continued to generate his computer instructions. He continued to verbally assault; emotionally torment; and misuse and contort Scriptures to blame, shame, and manipulate Patty.

The marriage lasted five months.

* * *

Controllers come in all colors, shapes, sizes, in both sexes, and will take everything they can get. Most people will live with a controller for just so long, because after a while they realize they have been held hostage in their own home. Those who live in a home with a controlling person, and who choose to be controlled, will begin to hate the controller.

You married for partnership, but something went terribly wrong. One day you woke up to the realization that you had become nothing more than a peasant in a dictatorship.

Controllers may do to children everything they are doing to their mate—and more. They may impose their dictatorial style on them with even greater intensity, assuming that they are powerless to retaliate. Living under this type of regime, the likelihood of your children ever being able to leave home as responsible adults is almost nil. Most likely they will remain enmeshed with the controller for years, trying to gain the approval they never felt. Or they will feel compelled to escape for the relief they need so badly from the wearing agenda of the controller.

THE MAKING OF A CONTROLLER

Why would someone be so controlling of others?

Controllers are people who, as children, often felt out of control because they were surrounded by chaos. They learned to survive by taking charge. All children see themselves as the center of the universe. The young believe they are responsible for all that occurs. They are self-centered. If things around them are out of control, especially parents, children will elect themselves the leader. They truly believe they can make the difference and bring order to the chaos.

Of course they cannot. Instead, they create an *illusion* of power and effectiveness. They think, distortedly, that they are in control. 1 Corinthians 13:11 addresses this very phenomenon: "When I was a child, I spoke like a child, I thought like a child, I reasoned like a child; when I became a man, I gave up childish ways" (RSV). We know from the study of behavior in psychology that a child's reasoning is self-centered. It is also emotionally based, because children have not accumulated the knowledge or the experience to make wiser, more informed decisions. The illusion of control, while believable to the child, remains only an illusion when viewed at a distance from the perspective of an adult.

As an adult, the controller is usually still practicing the survival and coping strategies that he or she developed as a child. Unfortunately, the behaviors have frequently gone unchallenged. The controller, therefore, remains unaware that his or her behaviors are ineffective in reaching the most important goals at which they are aimed: to bring harmony and love to replace the pain and emptiness he or she has endured.

In dealing with controllers, we need to be careful to distinguish between the person and the behavior—behavior which is at best irritating, and at most highly intolerable and offensive. The controller needs our compassion.

On the other hand, compassion for the controller does not mean submitting to his or her behavior. Christ always felt love and compassion for people, but that did not mean he tolerated sinful behavior. He refused, for instance, to tolerate the money changers in the temple. There are explanations for controlling behavior, but there are no justifications. The Bible never condones any behavior simply because it is a product of past victimization or mistreatment.

Let's look further at some causes and consequences of controlling behavior.

1. **Selfishness.** Let's face it! Some people are just "ME FIRST"! They view kindness as a weakness. Power, fame, wealth, and sensual gratification are satisfactions not to be postponed, but to be granted immediately and repeatedly on demand. *Distorted thinking leads these individuals to love things and use people.*

2. **Shame.** On the outside, controllers appear to be bullies or intimidators. Yet, on the inside, controllers are desperately trying to make the outside world conform to their own distorted sense of order. They need to look good, be competent, and create perfection around them because they feel so unacceptable and flawed within themselves. What a painful way to live! Neither the controller nor the people around them usually understand the purpose of their offensive actions. Everyone gets hurt. Everyone suffers. According to Janet G. Woititz, in *Struggle for Intimacy*, controllers

believe: "If I am not in complete control at all times, there will be anarchy."*

People suffering from shame convince themselves that their controlling behavior is necessary to themselves and to others for maintaining order. They spend a great deal of energy protecting themselves from actually feeling their deepest emotions. They ward off feelings of vulnerability, inadequacy, and fear by distracting themselves. They are about everyone else's business, and looking for what others and their environment can do to make them feel good. The flaws of others serve as a curtain behind which to hide their own flaws. The controlling behavior is a mask for their fear of confronting themselves or being revealed as inadequate. They fear facing their shame and are consumed with keeping this feeling at bay. Their emotional stability depends on their remaining in control—and they are experts at it.

John Bradshaw writes:

Control is a major cover up for toxic shame. Control is a product of grandiosity and distorts thinking in two ways: You see yourself as *helpless* and externally controlled or as omnipotent and responsible for everyone around you. You don't believe that you have any real control over the outcome of your life. This keeps you stuck and in your shame cycle. The opposite fallacy is the fallacy of *omnipotent control.* You feel responsible for everything and everybody. You carry the world on your shoulders and feel guilty when it doesn't work out.**

3. Fear and insecurity. Controllers are usually perfectionists. Due to their toxic shame, controllers cannot tolerate mistakes in anyone, including themselves, because those mis-

---

* Janet G. Woititz, *Struggle for Intimacy* (Deerfield Beach, Fla.: Health Communications, 1985), 51.
** John Bradshaw, *Healing the Shame that Binds You* (Deerfield Beach, Fla.: Health Communications, 1988), 197.

takes may somehow reflect on them. Controllers fear criticism, an arrow that strikes right at the heart of perfection. The people close to controllers (mate and children) are prime targets for the controller's fear and intolerance of criticism. Controllers will try to suppress any perceived imperfection in the mate's and children's behavior.

4. Modeling. Today's controllers are yesterday's children of controllers. People tend to duplicate the behavior of their parents, even though they themselves were emotionally or physically injured by those controlling behaviors. Regardless of what we have observed and experienced in life, however, we have no excuse for imposing abusive or oppressive control over another. "Monkey see, monkey do" refers to monkeys. As humans, we have a choice. We are individually fully responsible and accountable for those choices.

5. Distorted theology. Controllers who are Christians often use Scripture to defend their behavior, as did Bruce in the introductory story. But what appears to be biblical and spiritual is just another tool to force others to serve the desires of the controller. Even good things like the Bible can be used to do evil. Controllers rationalize and convince themselves that they are correctly interpreting Scripture, while they use it to manipulate others. Jesus used Scripture to clarify, but never to manipulate. Controllers have superior and blaming attitudes. This in no way depicts the attitude of one who is committed to the truths and ways of God. There is nothing spiritual about arrogance.

6. Enough is never enough! Controllers often suffer from character disorders such as a borderline or narcissistic personality disorder. Explained simply, the borderline personality is marked by a deep feeling of emptiness. The narcissistic personality is marked by an enormously inflated view of self-importance. The controller with either of these disorders is insatiable: Borderline controllers always remain empty; narcissistic controllers always believe they deserve more— more than they have, more than you have, more than anyone has.

These character disorders also involve delusions, which means these people are incapable of reasoning. You'll never win an argument with these people, and never convince them of your viewpoints. The egocentric quality of a child now resides in an adult body. We understand the natural self-centeredness of a child, therefore we instruct and guide them, and generally observe growth over time. In an adult, egocentricity makes for predictably painful and demanding interaction.

7. **Man-haters, woman-haters.** Many of us have experienced difficult and painful relationships in our lives. Some have left scars so deep that we want revenge. Women who have been hurt by men often feel anger toward all men. Of course, the same is true of men deeply hurt or injured by women. This generalization to an entire gender leads to extreme distortions and inappropriate responses. Controllers, remember, are protecting themselves from becoming vulnerable. The greater the previous injuries, the greater the perceived need to control.

ARE YOU A CONTROLLER?

Now that we have described the characteristics of and reasons for controlling behavior, it's time for you to assess whether you are a controlling person. Read each of the following statements, and check any that you would answer yes to:

1. _____ Have your mate or children grown exceedingly quiet in your presence?

2. ____ Do you have devoted, long-term friendships with people of the same sex?

3. ____ Do you find yourself uncomfortable when people—especially your spouse—make decisions which will affect you directly (accepting social invitations, planning meals, loaning possessions)?

4. ____ Do you find that most of the discretionary income (spending money) in your budget is used to purchase items for your personal pleasure, or for things you have unilaterally decided to be "essential"?

5. ____ Do you rarely, if ever, ask for and follow the advice or opinion of your mate?

6. ____ Do you believe that you are more in tune with the will of God than is your mate?

7. ____ Do you spend time pursuing mostly your own interests rather than considering and participating in your mate's interests?

8. ____ Do you get irritated when a routine schedule changes (dinner time, weekend plans, holiday plans)?

9. ____ Are you more aware of your mate's imperfections than of your own?

10. ____ Would you say that you can't count on your mate to get things done? If you want them done, or done right, do you have to do them yourself?

11. ____ Do you experience personality conflicts with people in positions of authority more than most people do?

12. ___ Do you find that you have short, rather than long, exchanges of conversation with your mate and children?

13. ___ Do you find that you must interrogate your mate or children just to keep things on track? ("Whom did you talk to, what did you say?")

14. ___ Do you feel a general sense of dissatisfaction with your mate most of the time?

15. ___ Do you like dogs better than cats?

16. ___ Is your favorite breed of dog the pit bull?

17. ___ Do you get a tinge of satisfaction at the thought of people fearing or being intimidated by you?

18. ___ Would you admit that you harbor strong prejudices against people of a different gender, race, class, political persuasion, or religion?

19. ___ Do you insist on being the driver rather than the passenger in a car whenever possible?

20. ___ Do you find it irritating to teach your mate or child?

While many people would check a couple of these questions, because on occasion they were true about them, the controller would check most of the questions, and they would be true for him or her much of the time.

ARE YOU LIVING WITH A CONTROLLER?

If you are not a controller, you may be living with one. Here's another list of questions, to help you assess your mate's control tendencies. Again, check the following questions to which you would answer yes.

1. ____ Do you feel your mate's need to be right is considerably greater than your own need to be right?

2. ____ Do you dread the time you spend with your mate?

3. ____ Do you measure your words to avoid upsetting your mate?

4. ____ Do you feel devalued by your mate?

5. ____ Would you say your mate treats you like a child, often interrupting, correcting, or instructing you?

6. ____ Does your mate point out your shortcomings and flaws on a regular basis?

7. ____ When your mate is criticized, does he or she overreact?

8. ____ Does your mate resent your friends and the time you spend with them?

9. ____ Do you rarely spend time with your individual friends?

10. ____ Have you lost confidence in your own abilities and judgment?

11. ____ Do you feel an obligation to consult your mate before making decisions of small consequence?

12. ____ Do you often fantasize about running away?

13. ____ Have you ever compared your life to being in prison?

14. ____ Do you feel trapped?

15. ____ Do you love cats? Do you see them as misunderstood?

16. ____ Do you often wish you had never married?

17. ____ Are most of your possessions old and worn out as a result of your mate controlling the finances?

18. ____ Do you work to avoid being at home?

19. ____ Do you feel like a peasant working for a dictator?

20. ____ In relation to your mate, do you feel used more often than you feel loved?

If you feel you have lost yourself in your marriage, or wish you had never married, you need help. We recommend you seek professional or pastoral counseling to assess the situation. Whatever you do, continuing in your current pattern will never lead to resolution. It will most likely get worse.

To the pastor. If you encounter emotional or physical abuse, refer the couple to a professional counselor unless you have special expertise in the area. If you do have expertise, and you choose to counsel this specialized population, you may have to turn to the church body to assist you in keeping the abusive person accountable. We recommend that churches require a lot of accountability from members who abuse their spouses and children. Do not be blinded by gender. Do not minimize the signs and complaints of abuse and domestic violence.

To the controller or the controlled. If you can admit that you are either very controlling or very controlled, you have reached a crossroads. The important question before you is whether or not you will attempt to restore and preserve your marriage relationship. The road less traveled, the high road, would be to make every effort to work through what may seem to be insurmountable. By no means would you be expected to walk this journey alone. Help is essential. Recognizing that it takes courage and perseverance, we strongly recommend you reach out to competent support as you assess your unique situation.

A success story. A promising future seemed to await Bob and Colleen as they walked down the aisle. Bob was gentle, kind, and thoughtful. He often sought opportunities to help a neighbor or a friend stuck in the middle of a difficult project. Everyone liked Bob. He was chosen Teacher of the Year at the junior high where he taught. Bob's strong points were also his weak points. As has often been observed, any strength taken to the extreme can become a weakness. Bob tended to promote others at the expense of himself, creating a vacuum of unmet needs deep inside him.

Colleen was also a teacher, beloved by both her students and peers. She was by everybody's definition an extrovert. To her, any social setting was an opportunity for stand-up comedy. Colleen was also a natural-born leader. She, too, had been voted Teacher of the Year at her school.

Bob and Colleen were opposites. Their personalities complemented each other in many areas. As the years of their marriage grew from one to ten, a pattern evolved. What had appeared to be complementary differences had created a subtle erosion in their marriage, but *harm can result from even the best of intentions.*

Colleen was an expert storyteller, and she knew it. Often, when Bob began to tell a story familiar to both of them, she would jump in and say, "Bob, let me tell the story. I'll tell it better!" Invariably, Bob acquiesced as Colleen enthralled the audience with her artful storytelling. Colleen interpreted Bob's tendency to defer as permission and approval to become increasingly assertive. Neither Bob nor Colleen realized it, but a deep well of emptiness began to grow inside him. In social circles Bob began to think of himself as uninteresting and unimportant. He came to the point where he could not break the frustrating pattern he had unwittingly established.

By the tenth year of their marriage, Bob had become resentful of Colleen's intrusions into his conversations. Yet he did not make a single attempt to change the pattern. He never mentioned his frustration to Colleen. Eventually, he began to avoid her and didn't like to hear others acclaim her engaging personality and wit. In social settings, he would seat himself against back walls away from Colleen, or migrate to a separate room. At times, a nauseating feeling resulted from the anger that was welling up inside him.

Bob's habit of deferring to Colleen invaded all areas of their marriage. Although she sensed Bob's increasing withdrawal, Colleen still concluded that she and Bob were content with each other. She had rationalized to herself that everything was okay.

Neither Bob nor Colleen knew that their marriage was hanging by a slender thread. The day came when the thread was severed in a most unusual way. It was during the era when men and women tightly permed their hair. Colleen made the decision to have hers permed and casually mentioned this to Bob. Bob rarely argued strongly about anything, but that night he begged her not to change her hair. He emphatically explained that he liked her hair the way it was and *hated* permed hair. But Colleen kept her appointment at the hair salon. Her arrival home marked a turning point in their marriage. Although Bob's anger boiled inside him, his only words were, "You had to do it, didn't you!" He walked to the closet, grabbed a suitcase and filled it with enough clothes to get him through the weekend. Colleen stood in stunned silence. Bob's parting words in no way stated the depth of anger he was feeling. He only said, "I have to get out of here for a while."

The *while* turned into a six-month separation. Bob had determined to completely avoid direct contact with Colleen and for six long months they did not have any direct conversation.

Colleen was baffled by Bob's reaction. Upset and confused, she called her closest friend. Ashley had far greater insight into Bob's reaction, having observed their marital relationship for years. In the tradition of a faithful friend, Ashley told Colleen the painful truth. "Colleen, your problem is that you never learned when to shut up! For ten years I have watched you dominate every conversation I have witnessed. I never saw you allow Bob to finish a good story or to fully develop an opinion on any important topic. I never called you on it, because Bob didn't seem to mind."

Colleen was still perplexed. She rebutted, "But that has nothing to do with it. Bob just left because I got my hair permed. I just don't get it!"

Undaunted by Colleen's confusion, Ashley continued, "If Bob said he hated perms, why did you rush out and get one? Don't you see that was a slap in the face to him? He hardly ever tells you what he is thinking! This time he begged you. Instead of taking him seriously, you ignored him."

Ashley's words convicted her. Colleen had turned a deaf ear to her husband's protests. She had become callous to his feelings.

Ashley did not hesitate. "It wouldn't hurt to apologize.

And, you might think about having your hair straightened as soon as possible."

Colleen hastened to write an apologetic and thoughtful note to Bob, and within a few days she returned to the beauty salon to straighten her permed hair. Sadly, days turned into weeks and months before Bob responded in any way to her note. For six months, they communicated only in writing. These notes were limited to business matters and household repairs. Like ships passing in the night, Bob would only come to the house if Colleen was at work or was gone from the premises.

One day, by accident, they met face-to-face. Colleen had returned home unexpectedly to pick up an item she had forgotten, just as Bob had arrived to repair a plumbing problem. Speaking a soft hello, Colleen managed a brief, contrite smile. Bob was immediately struck with the realization that Colleen's hair was back to her normal style. In almost a whisper, he haltingly asked, "Colleen, did you do that for me?"

Through her tears Colleen replied, "Yes, Bob. I changed it back for you six months ago. I never meant to hurt you. I can't believe how blind I was. I never dreamed we would end up like this. I'm so sorry."

Bob began to weep. He felt overwhelmed with confusion. He longed to work out the problems of their marriage, but was afraid of losing his personality to Colleen again. He wanted to do the right thing, but his confidence had been shattered. He had spent six months asking himself if there was any real hope of repairing the relationship. Could they ever recapture the love they once shared? Would the past wounds heal, only to resurface once they were together? What were the answers? Bob wanted to do the right thing. He chose to do the right thing... he chose to take the road less traveled.

Bob made an appointment with a pastoral counselor, who skillfully offered him the hope that a solid relationship could be renegotiated. Now, filled with hope, Bob invited Colleen to join him in the counselor's office. They explored the path that had led to their separation. *They gained insight and took personal responsibility for the roles they had played.* Both had contributed to the breakdown. Each would have to change. They were offered specific methods and tools to repair and reconcile the broken relationship. They were counseled to understand that change requires ongoing discipline and commitment. By word and action, they each accepted the assignment.

Several months later Bob and Colleen were having dinner with a friend. Bob began to tell a story. Colleen, excited about the story, attempted to fill in the details as would a color commentator. Bob looked lovingly at her and said, "Colleen, you're doing it again." Her face flushed red for a brief moment, and she said, "I'm sorry, Bob." Bob finished the story and later explained to his friend that the counselor had suggested he use the phrase "You're doing it again" to cue Colleen when she was invading an area that was important to his self-respect.

Colleen had found the secret to what the Bible calls meekness. Meekness is best defined as *strength under control.* All those years, Bob and Colleen had the power to build a team in which each could flourish without diminishing either of their personalities. However, while they had the power, they lacked the insight and the tools. In the past, Colleen had not been aware of when to exercise her strength and when to make room for another. She now had learned to use her strength of personality in ways that enhanced others as well as herself. Bob had learned to take the initiative and to value his own contributions, rather than passively retreating. A mutual respect and appreciation was reborn in their marriage. Feeling a new freedom between them, on occasion Bob could be heard saying, "Colleen, why don't you tell the story; you tell it so much better."

The successful work Bob and Colleen did to rebuild their marriage effectively called attention to each of their contributions to the problem. Colleen had become a controller and Bob had allowed himself to be controlled. Bob willingly gave up his rights early in the marriage. Had he admitted much earlier that he was experiencing dark feelings, the marriage would not have reached such a dangerous level of pain. Had Colleen been more aware, she would have noticed a lack of sensitivity and regard toward her husband. Despite the fact that both people had loving and positive intentions, they had created patterns of interaction that eroded the marriage.

What about you?

We invite you to read ahead to gain instruction and insight to build a successful marriage where there may be a tendency or a prominent pattern of controlling behavior.

A CONTROLLER'S STEPS TOWARD CHANGE

Put simply, controllers need to let go of control. They need to realize that they are destroying the relationship they are desperately trying to keep. Controllers must turn their efforts away from control and toward love and respect. Failing to do so will leave nothing to preserve; they will inherit the wind.

But before controllers can change direction, they must have a change of heart. An essential first step is an open and humble attitude. The passion formerly used to control must be aimed at gaining understanding and showing consideration and love. With a tenacious motivation to change, the controller will be well on the way to transforming the destructive relationship pattern into quality and fulfilling interactions.

God is in the business of changing hearts. The most powerful tool he uses is his Word. Consider these pertinent instructions:

For everything that was written in the past was written to teach us, so that through endurance and the encouragement of the Scriptures we might have hope.   **Romans 15:4**

I pray that out of his glorious riches he may strengthen you with power through his Spirit in your inner being, so that Christ may dwell in your hearts through faith.

Ephesians 3:16-17

Behold, Thou dost desire truth in the innermost being,
And in the hidden part Thou wilt make me know wisdom.

Psalm 51:6 NKJV

When pride comes, then comes disgrace,
But with humility comes wisdom. **Proverbs 11:2**

Trust in the Lord with all your heart
and lean not on your own understanding;
in all your ways acknowledge him,
and he will make your paths straight. **Proverbs 3:5-6**

Work through the following steps to help identify the controlling behaviors you have been exercising in your marriage. This is an opportunity for you to gain insight into how your behavior is affecting your partner. It is also an opportunity for you to change.

1. Ask your mate to specifically share with you the ways he or she finds you to be controlling. Use the checklist on page 147 to help identify problem areas.

2. *Write down* what your partner says. Writing it down will reinforce your understanding and allow you to refer back if you need a refresher.

3. Give your mate the freedom to remind you when you have crossed the line. Your mate can best tell if he or she feels controlled.

4. When you learn you have crossed the line and controlled, apologize. Remember, you are working as a team to solve the problem.

5. Frequently ask your mate's opinion, and act upon it. This will return the credibility and self-respect that your previously controlling behavior stripped away from your mate.

6. If you blow it, regroup. When practicing something new, we all can use a little mercy! Marriage is not about winning and losing, or competition. Stand up, dust yourselves off, and get back in the game.

7. Frequently ask if your mate is feeling the freedom you intend to return to him or her. If the answer is no, don't become defensive. Instead, listen and heed the cue to change your behavior. If your mate says he or she feels controlled by you, trust that feedback. Your mutual respect and cooperation will transform your relationship into a God-designed marriage.

William Wordsworth said, "The best portions of a man's life are his little, nameless, unremembered acts of kindness and of love." How true that is of men, women, and children. Nothing touches us more deeply, or heals our souls, like kindness.

IF YOU ARE CONTROLLED...

People who have allowed someone else to control them need to regain their self-respect and self-control. They must come to grips with the reality that as long as they endure and accept it, the oppressive cycle will continue. Francis Schaeffer stated this principle simply as he declared to thousands in stadiums around the United States, *"We get what we tolerate."*

People who are controlled by others need to learn how to

build boundaries to protect themselves from intolerable behaviors. If you don't establish some boundaries in your present relationship, you are doomed to repeat the same patterns in future relationships. You have nothing to lose and everything to gain by facing this problem.

You will need spiritual encouragement. These Scripture verses are fuel for the soul:

When anxiety was great within me,
your consolations brought joy to my soul.   **Psalm 94:19**

Come to Me, all you who are weary and burdened,
and I will give you rest.   **Matthew 11:28**

The Lord is close to the brokenhearted,
and saves those who are crushed in spirit.   **Psalm 34:18**

By day the Lord commands his steadfast love;
and at night his song is with me,
a prayer to the God of my life.   **Psalm 42:8 RSV**

Here is a list of steps to help you and your mate address the issue of control in your relationship:

1. Offer constructive and specific feedback to your mate about the offensive actions and the impact they have on you.

2. Offer suggestions for more loving and positive substitutes for the controlling behaviors. For example, "In the future I would prefer..." or, "I would respond positively to..."

3. Trust is earned. It will take time and patience to rebuild the trust.

4. Take notice of your boundaries. If your mate steps over the

line into the control area, alert him with a gentle cue. For example, "I feel stepped on. I would prefer..." or, "You're doing it again" (said with an attitude of kindness, of course!).

5. If the controller doesn't heed the cue, take action to protect yourself from further offense. "Because you are continuing to..., I am choosing to leave the room." Do not allow the destructive process to continue. Take charge of yourself by making an alternate choice for yourself. This is what boundaries and self-respect require.

6. Recognize and affirm your partner's attitudes and attempts to change.

7. Love expects the best. Your expectant posture will foster growth in your controlling mate if he or she is sincerely endeavoring to change. (Rejection is not a catalyst for growth.)

These steps provide a road map. We highly recommend counseling for both the controller and the controlled. It is not easy to make the transition from the painful experience you are living, to proceed into these more healthy steps. While you may be able to make headway on your own, support can ease the process. For many, the recommended steps will be unreachable without outside support. Support can make all the difference.*

---

*A word of caution for pastoral and professional counselors:** If you are counseling a couple in an abusive relationship and have tried to provide counsel and have worked through the process (perhaps even repeatedly) without success, the controller is not cooperating. Do not continue trying to reconcile a couple in a continuously abusive relationship. If you are tempted to ask a severely controlled and abused mate to wait for a miracle, remember that, by nature, miracles rarely happen. If they happened often, they wouldn't be called miracles.

The cure rate for *physically* abusive persons, even when counseled, is only about 3 percent. So think twice before asking a woman (or man) to remain in a physically abusive situation. God is our Father; we can only imagine the grief that this unwise or uninformed counsel would bring to him regarding his beloved children. On the other hand, what an opportunity to protect those he loves from unnecessary pain. "In as much as you have done it unto the least of these my brethren, you have done it unto me" (Matthew 25:40 NKJV).

TWELVE

⌒

Keeping In-Laws in Line

C an you imagine Adam saying to Eve, "Do you remember when I was a little boy?" Of course not! Adam was never a little boy, nor a baby, nor an adolescent. He was created as a full-grown, adult male, and Eve was a full-grown female. Have you ever wondered about the life of this first couple? Have you ever imagined that, in some orchid-filled glade nestled in the Garden of Eden, there was a marriage ceremony, with the animals attending to pay homage to their king and queen? We don't know if there was such a ceremony, but we do know God's first words to this fascinating couple.

Picture Adam, standing regal and tall, with Eve by his side, pure and matchless in beauty. Filled with reverence and interest they waited to hear what the Creator would say. The Lord looked at them and spoke emphatically,

> For this reason a man will leave his father and mother and be united to his wife, and they will become one flesh.
>
> **Genesis 2:24**

Had Gary been the minister performing Adam and Eve's wedding, his words would have been considerably more romantic. He might have been compelled to say, "This day is the beginning of a union never before experienced in the universe. You will be the very first to drink the joys of the deep, fulfilling romance that you were designed for by God himself. What an honor to be the model for all people! By the way, those soft folds under your nose that rest on your teeth are called lips. Kiss a lot! You'll like it. The appendages that dangle from your shoulders are arms. Use them often, mostly for hugging. It's their highest calling, you see! There are a few other body parts you will discover along the way. You are pre-programmed to figure them out. Enjoy!"

With all that God might have said, he opted for two points in his message to this first couple:

1. Marriage is not a relationship destined for mediocrity. It is to be a united and intimate relationship, more intimate than any other relationship.

2. The marriage relationship is to be the most important of all human relationships—even more important than that of children and parents.

It is fascinating to note that God directs the man and woman to leave their parents, when in fact the couple he is talking to have no parents to leave! God intends for Adam and Eve to teach their children to eventually become independent from *their* parents (Adam and Eve!). Furthermore, he intends for them to help their children become independent from them in a specific area—in matters of relationship. Did you ever wonder about God's timing in giving this first instruction?

God knew that children would soon be born to Adam and Eve. And *God knew* the significance of the role all human parents would play in the lives of their children. After all, he designed the parent-child relationship. *God knew* from the beginning what modern psychology has just recently tapped into: What parents do to their children, say to their children, and model for their children affects the children's lives until the day they die. From our parents we learn to trust, we learn what is funny, what has value. We learn how to react to adversity. From our parents we learn discipline, responsibility, and what it means to be male or female. It would be difficult to overestimate the impact our parents have on our lives. And *God knew* that from the beginning.

God knew also that Adam and Eve would become fallen creatures. They would be tempted to hold on all too selfishly to the things that belong to God—including their very children. Thus, his first words to this first couple now make more sense.

Consider this affirmation from Scripture:

> Moreover, we have all had human fathers who disciplined us and we respected them for it. How much more should we submit to the Father of our spirits and live! Our fathers disciplined us for a little while as they thought best; but God disciplines us for our good, that we may share in his holiness.   **Hebrews 12:9-10**

This verse underscores the limits of parental control. Parental control has a beginning and an end, as indicated by the phrase *"for a little while."* When control continues for a long time, it becomes unnatural, falling outside of God's plan for marriage.

In Ephesians 5:31, Paul repeats for the adult community in the church at Ephesus God's charge to Adam and Eve:

> For this reason a man will leave his father and mother and be united to his wife, and the two will become one flesh.

Again, we are talking to parents, not children. It is the parents' responsibility to slowly let go of their children as they prepare to live independent lives. The very parental authority and leadership that was necessary and appropriate earlier in the game no longer fits. The parents make a role transition from *parents of children* to *parents of adults.* New roles, new rules.

If parents either haven't learned this truth, or are unskilled or unwilling to apply it, their adult offspring will have to initiate the changes. It becomes the unnatural yet necessary task of the young adult children to claim freedom and independence from the inappropriate control and influence of their parents.

It is not dishonoring to your parents to claim this separateness if they refuse to obey the admonition given twice by God, once in the Garden of Eden and once through Paul in Ephesians. From the beginning, the goal of the parent was clearly established: *Prepare your children to become truly independent, responsible, and free.*

The parent-child relationship has a major impact on the future marriage of the offspring. Scripture has many great illustrations involving parent-child relationships. Allow us to use three to illustrate what God had in mind and what he didn't have in mind.

1. The Prodigal Son. In the story of the Prodigal Son (Luke 15:11-32) we find a father (who represents God) allowing his adult son to make his own decisions. The decisions are costly and wrong, nevertheless they were his adult decisions. Because of his upbringing, the son finally comes around. He learns to make sound judgments, but only after he has seriously failed on his own. Would you accuse the father of irresponsibility? I think not! He understood the son's need to become his own person, and the son's return is all the more meaningful because he wanted to come back and was not manipulated to do so.

It was a grace-based relationship. This is, of course, what God had in mind for all relationships, especially that of parent and child. The best part of the story occurs at the end: The son comes home wiser, with his individuality intact. His character has been strengthened, as evidenced by his humble attitude.

2. Saul and Jonathan. In the case of Saul and Jonathan, the father fails to let his son go, but the son succeeds in claiming his independence. Saul tries in every way possible to interfere with Jonathan's relationship with David, but Jonathan establishes and maintains his boundaries with his obsessively controlling father. Although Saul makes a case, appealing for Jonathan's loyalty (as defined by Saul), Jonathan is able to clearly see that his friendship with David and his loyalty to his father need not conflict. This is a matter of principle for Jonathan. He is even asked to kill his friend, David. He knows that killing him would be sinful and drastic. He refuses to participate in the evil. If we are loyal to our principles, dealing with people's demands will not confuse our loyalties. Through it all, Jonathan honors Saul as his father.

3. **Jacob.** The story of Jacob is crawling with parents and children who are enmeshed in the worst possible ways. First of all, Jacob is what we call a momma's boy. Rebecca has him wrapped around her little finger so tightly that Jacob willingly enters into a plot to deceive his own father, whose favor he has never enjoyed. That's because his father, Isaac, loves Jacob's twin brother, Esau, much more than he loves Jacob. Esau is given all the approval, to the point of being spoiled. Jacob's need to be blessed by his father is tremendous and lingering. The manipulations of his mother nearly ruin his life. He dies an unhappy man after confessing to the Pharaoh of Egypt, "Few and miserable have been the days and years of my life."

It didn't help things when Jacob married the daughters of a manipulating and controlling father named Laban. Jacob ultimately had to cut him completely out of the family.

It is a wonder that, given the problems Jacob and Rachel had in their families of origin, they were able to produce a Joseph, one of the greatest and most balanced men who ever lived. Joseph's story is good news for sons and daughters of controlling parents. The story teaches that it is possible to break the chain. Jonathan did it and Joseph did it. And we can do it, too.

In Jacob's story we see the two causes of enmeshed relationships. The first cause is strong but manipulative parents.

The second cause is parents who never allow their children to feel approved, so that the children never feel ready to move away from home even if they have to. Sometimes a physical separation occurs, but the emotional enmeshment remains, regardless of the actual physical distance. A person may still be enmeshed though their parents are dead. The controlling ties between a parent and child can be so strong that the deceased parent has no problem whatsoever reaching right out of the grave to make his or her child's life miserable. Sometimes, for the sake of a marriage, a couple may have to exorcise a ghost from their home.

LIVING WITH A GHOST?

Alex and Amy experienced the drama of living with a ghost. Alex reminded Amy of her father. He had the same charcoal hair, the same strong jaw line, identical deep-set blue eyes. Besides a similar appearance, there was a similar intellectual style, love for music and a compelling sense of humor. Just like her father, Jack, Amy's husband was usually the life of the party. Amy's memory of her father was her most cherished possession. His untimely death was redeemed when she met Alex. She had an immediate and magnetic attraction to Alex.

Alex had fallen into a spiderweb! He was the prey. Amy attempted in every way possible to conform Alex to substitute for her father. Jack was, in fact, as wonderful as she had remembered. A man of stature, integrity, and family devotion. A man who met no strangers. There was no way to number the times he had held Amy in his arms to comfort her, as a child and as a young woman.

His timely words filled the darkest moments with light. Amy had clear memories of his wisdom-filled eyes, always beholding her with love and understanding. Best of all, her father always treated her mother with tender love and respect. He was emotionally present, responsible, and an incredible provider. Ozzie

Nelson, Ward Cleaver, and Jim Anderson could have taken lessons from Jack. This seasoned man was a tough act to follow for a young, well-meaning, and loving husband. In fact, he was an impossible act to follow.

What made it even more hopeless was that Amy idealized this fine image of her father. She never grieved his death. Instead, she mentally wrapped him in ribbons and put him on a pedestal which would serve as her measure of all men. Even Jack himself couldn't have competed with the monument that she had erected in her mind! What hope could there be for young Alex?

From the beginning, Alex was flooded with the refrain, "Daddy did this," and, "Daddy did that." But it didn't stop there. Besides all the verbal comparing and one-upping, she privately expected that Alex would never meet her expectations. The race was over before it began. The marriage ended abruptly when Alex found in his workplace a woman who thought him rather special. Need we say more?

Amy committed a common mistake: She fell into the trap of comparing her mate to someone else instead of relating to her mate as he was. Because of this, instead of deepening a bond with her marriage partner by experiencing his uniqueness, she alienated him. Her bond was with her father only. She left no room for Alex to grow closer to her. Furthermore, she set her expectations on Alex becoming like her father, a role Alex could never fulfill. He became frustrated and lonely and sought comfort from another woman who appreciated him as he was.

ARE VIPERS LETHAL?

Enmeshment with parents can have many faces. In the next account we witness the horrifying bite of a viper:

As a high school senior, David was voted most likely to succeed. He did succeed, in every area except his first marriage.

He married the sophomore class princess in his junior year of college at Boston University. Kim came from "old money," and her relatives' footprints could be found all over Plymouth Rock. Kim's mother can only be described as pompous, arrogant, and controlling. She played to the audience and expected her daughter to always uphold the family name. Her mother embraced a fear early in Kim's life, a fear that would haunt Kim and become the source of deep and ongoing pain. Simply stated, that fear was, *Nobody will ever be good enough for my daughter.* From the beginning of David and Kim's relationship, Kim's mother found ways to undermine David's character.

She criticized his honorable, "blue-collar" family. She even discredited the full academic scholarships he earned that carried him right through medical school. She repeatedly begged Kim to note that David did not own the kind of ambition that would take him to the top. She went so far as to draw Kim's attention to trivial matters such as the shape of David's nose, his receding hairline, how his ears stood out slightly from his head, and his rather average height of 5'10".

In the beginning, Kim's love for David weathered the criticism. But when Kim took employment to help David complete medical school, their relationship took a dangerous downward turn. Between David's part-time employment and Kim's full-time employment, combined with the late hours of study, they had become strangers. The only input Kim was getting was from her mother. Rather than talking with David about her loneliness, she opted to listen to relentless and cruel attacks from her mother against every aspect of David's being.

David was completely unaware of these frequent "David-bashings." When he saw Kim's mother, she acted proper, as one would expect. No one was more surprised than David when Kim announced that she was filing for divorce. It took years before he was able to understand the process that led to the failure of his marriage and what he and Kim could have done to prevent it.

IF THINGS ARE SO GOOD,
THEN WHY DO I FEEL SO BAD?

The following scenario is typical of most young couples who seek counseling regarding in-law problems:

Tamara's dark, penetrating eyes were evidence of the sensitive, intellectual woman she had grown to be. She had been watching Nick for two years. The fears she experienced as a fiancée grew into nightmares when she became Nick's bride. Before marriage, she had often wondered if Nick was more closely tied to his parents than was appropriate for a husband. Today, she no longer had to wonder.

What seemed like an endearing gesture had become completely threatening. Each and every day, when Nick came home from work at 6:30 P.M., he walked straight to the phone to call his mother. It was more than a habit. It was a ritual. What made it worse was that he would make the call before showing any kind of interest or attention to Tamara or their nine-month-old daughter, Nicole. Worse still, he was now making the call from their bedroom and speaking in whispers, completely excluding his wife from the conversations.

If his contacts with his parents had energized him, making him more affectionate and alive to their relationship, the phone calls would have been a welcome addition to their marriage. But Nick would emerge withdrawn, defensive, and depressed. Tamara was building a mountain of resentment inside.

Usually after these calls, Nick could be seen sprawling on the couch watching TV, rather than processing his day with Tamara, playing with Nicole, or otherwise being involved in the inviting young family life they had created together.

Tamara had become painfully aware that visiting her own family was not a welcome option. If her parents were to see Nicole, she had to slip away during the week, making excuses explaining why they were never available on the weekends—

they were never available because Nick always had a felt need to spend time with his own parents, usually at their request.

During the visits to Nick's parents, Tamara was made to feel like an indulged guest, more than part of the family. She knew that her opinion was not valued. What irritated her most were the attempts of Nick's mother to "educate" her in the finer points of child-rearing. Nicole was happy and healthy, but Tamara never came away from the weekend visits with any sense of competence as a young mother. She felt she was the object of Nick's parents' criticism, both when she was with them and when she wasn't.

One day, during a candid moment, Tamara asked Nick if he felt that his parents were proud of him. His response amazed her: "I'm not sure I've ever done anything right in my life." Tamara thought for a moment, and then said, "Nick, that must be extremely painful. Why do you spend so much time with your parents when you are not ever sure that they are happy with who you are?"

Nick sighed and continued, "I know this sounds stupid, but I keep hoping that someday they will tell me I've done something right. I would like my mom or dad to tell me they are proud of my promotions. When I was in college, it was my grades. When I was in high school, it was my appearance. When I was in elementary school, it was my sports. To tell you the truth, Tamara, I can't give you a good answer to your question because I don't know why I want to spend so much time with my parents—since I always leave feeling demoralized."

Tamara smiled compassionately and spoke kindly, "Nick, I feel bad that you don't feel close to your parents. But to tell you the truth, I had begun to think I was doing something wrong and you were mad at me. I need to be honest and tell you that I have come to resent your parents' influence on our marriage, because I long to have the attention that I have seen you give to your mother. I want to be cherished, but I often feel in some ways like *you* feel when you're with your parents. I think we can fix this, but maybe we need some help. If you've been feeling this since childhood, chances are it's more complicated than it appears. I would love to give you the approval you have missed from your parents, but I don't think you will be able to receive it while you are still longing for theirs. Nick, I don't know how this will sound, but I think we need to get your parents out of our marriage. Not out of our lives, but out of our marriage."

TIME TO EVALUATE

How can you recognize parent-child enmeshment in your own marriage?

1. The enmeshed partner tends to value the opinions of his or her parents over the opinions of the mate.

2. The enmeshed partner feels uncomfortable making major decisions without first obtaining approval and permission from his or her parents.

3. The enmeshed partner feels obligated to accommodate the parents' schedule over the schedule of his or her mate.

4. The enmeshed partner obtains comfort from his or her parents when there is conflict in the marriage, rather than working things out with the mate. (This always leads to major complications: It is a *danger zone!*)

5. The enmeshed partner often views himself as a mediator, a "go-between," between the mate and parents. He is trying to keep the peace between the wrong people. This, again, is a *danger zone.* The end result is always the same: Neither

the mate nor the parents are pleased, making the situation more difficult than it was before the enmeshed partner dove into the middle.

6. The enmeshed partner will tend to establish an unnatural relationship with his or her own children. The unmet emotional needs in the partner may be met in the once natural, intimate relationship of the child. Only, the care-giving is working backwards. The care-giving is going from the child to the parent, because the parent needs affection from the child for emotional stability. The child's needs are no longer the focus. The hurting parent is trying to feel better and the intuitive child can feel it. The child makes the reverse care-giving switch very readily, because he or she feels the parent's pain deeply. Taken to the extreme, this would be an overwhelmingly suffocating experience for a child who feels responsible for the happiness of the parent.

7. The enmeshed partner will stop trusting. Both partners will be suspicious of each other's motives. They will begin second-guessing, demanding, and manipulating. No longer will they "expect the best" from each other (1 Corinthians 13: 7 LB). They may, in fact, expect the worst.

8. Partners enmeshed with parents or in-laws eventually become adversaries. The war is about to begin. *(The big danger zone!)*

Once the war begins, the couple will engage in any or all of the following:

1. Name calling, against mates and parents.

2. A growing perception of resentment and contempt.

3. Just when the wound begins to heal, a fresh attack comes from parent, in-laws, or mate. These make for roller-coaster encounters, with anger, threats, and making up.

4. Increased intensity in anger and emotional responses. Verbal abuse and physical violence may occur in some cases.

5. Insecurity mounts as each perceives the other as a threat. The insecurity fuels the anger and defensiveness.

WHERE DO WE GO FROM HERE?

Determine if you are involved in an enmeshed relationship with parents by completing the test below. It is most effective if both mates take the test. We recommend you take it separately, with an open mind.

Questionnaire for Enmeshment with Parents

1. ___ Do you or your mate feel an excessive need to obtain parental approval?

2. ___ Do you as marital partners often argue about decisions that involve your parents or in-laws or their opinions?

3. ___ Do your parents or in-laws make you feel guilty when you say no to their requests?

4. ___ Do your parents or in-laws make uncomfortable demands on your time?

5. ___ Do your parents or in-laws pre-plan your vacations, and feel hurt if you don't elect to join them?

6. __ Do these demands of your parents or in-laws lead to arguments and division in your marriage?

7. __ Have the arguments over parental or in-law involvement affected your sex life?

8. __ Do you experience fear and anxiety when you attempt to "interpret" your parents to your mate (i.e., "They didn't mean that; they mean this...")?

9. __ Would you say that you often feel "caught in the middle" between your mate and your mate's parents?

10. __ Has resentment built up so that you or your mate avoid talking about the other's parents? Is this a sore subject?

11. __ Does your mate defend his or her parents' opinions instead of upholding you or your opinion in the majority of situations that impact your marriage (e.g., finances, child-rearing styles, family gatherings, how to run a home)?

12. __ Do you feel devalued or betrayed as a result?

13. __ Do you feel like you are competing with your in-laws for your mate's affection?

14. __ Do you find yourself having dark thoughts regarding your in-laws? (Be honest.) If so, note the level of resentment that has built up.

Now that you have completed the test, let's be frank: If you answered yes to any of these questions, and these problems occur with much frequency, you have identified that you or your partner is enmeshed with parents. The "leaving and cleaving" process was not completed.

This means you have one foot at home with parents and the other foot in the marriage. (*Cleaving* means *to cherish or set apart into high value.* How virtuous that makes the marital relationship!) Regardless of how many years you have been married, it is now time to complete the natural separation process that God intended for everyone.

We want you to know there is hope. There is a way to change direction. You and your partner can make all the difference. (Note: If the pain and resentment are extreme and long-term, you may need a referee or professional help to facilitate the process. That's certainly a reasonable option.) With or without outside help, you can improve your situation by following the guidelines any counselor would suggest in this situation. We will explore one effective action plan.

THE ACTION PLAN STEP-BY-STEP

Here is a proven action plan for ending enmeshment with parents in a way that can lead to a renewed relationship for everyone:

1. Show consideration to all parties involved.
2. Admit that your mate's problem is your problem also.
3. Gain perspective.
4. Prepare to confront the issues.
5. Begin the process of confronting.
6. Troubleshoot (as necessary).

That's the six-step Action Plan in a nutshell. Now let's roll up our sleeves and explore the nitty-gritty of this process:

1. **Show consideration to all parties involved.** Everyone involved in an enmeshment relationship has tender feelings at stake. The enmeshment is most likely unintentional, even if it doesn't seem to be. It is our experience that most parents cooperate fully with the changes and healing process once they understand that they are having a negative effect on their child's marriage. Usually, their actions have been born out of love. Nevertheless, they have found themselves doing the wrong things for the right reasons. What we are saying is, cut your parents a little slack!

2. **Admit that your mate's problem is your problem also.** The two of you are one. This is *your* marriage. Take ownership of the problem. Put on the same uniform—you're on the same team. This action may be the most constructive step you have taken in your marriage for some time. Make it a habit. Confront the issues, not the people. You will discover what many people already know: Challenges and conflict present an opportunity to bond, to persist, and to grow closer.

3. **Gain perspective.** Set the problem at a distance from yourselves. Imagine the problem as an object, and imagine yourselves stepping a few stories above it. Look down on what should appear to be a much-reduced version of the issue. Then, with professional uniforms on, tackle the problem.

(**Important warning:** Do not proceed to action step 4 until successfully completing steps 1-3. If you cannot accomplish steps 1, 2, and 3, we advise you to meet with a facilitator such as a pastoral or professional counselor. If you proceed to action step 4 without completing the previous steps successfully, the confrontation will be destructive to all parties involved. It will only create a power struggle, not a peace treaty.)

Discouraged? Remember, wishing doesn't make it so. The enmeshment problem doesn't go away by itself. It must be worked through. Give yourself the freedom and support of having outside help for this involved process.

4. Prepare to confront the issues. Confrontation means to inform and clarify, not to start a fight. Without the necessary information, no one can make an appropriate change toward healthier interaction. Don't insulate yourselves from the problems. Educate. Educate yourselves. Educate your parents about the impact enmeshment is having on you and on them. This clarifying confrontation can be done with a hopeful and encouraging tone. Regardless of the level of pain and hurt caused by the enmeshment, your focus is on your hope that the future will be brighter, once you have taken the bull by the horns. Together, you can make a better plan.

5. Begin the process of confronting:

- Set the stage diplomatically. That can happen nicely if you begin by telling the in-laws or parents involved that you have a problem and they can help you solve it.

- Lovingly explain that your marriage has been affected by their behavior.

- Offer this olive branch: "We don't believe you have intentionally caused any of our pain."

- Tell them you are meeting together to clarify and inform, so that, in the future, contacts can be better.

- Explain very clearly that you have appreciated their involvement in your upbringing. Thank them specifically for things you learned from them, to emphasize that they are in no way total failures.

- Inform them that your greatest need is to claim your full independence from them in the sense of *"leaving and cleaving."*

- If there have been specific crossings of lines or boundaries into the marriage, this would be a good time to inform them of those occurrences and how they affected your marriage. Be clear, but not brutal.

- Let them know how they can be successful in their dealings with you in the future. Be specific. Example: *"That didn't work well for us because..." "In the future, we request that you..."*

- Allow the in-laws or parents to share the experience of enmeshment with you from their viewpoint. They also want to be understood, especially about their intentions. .

- Validate their good intentions. (Acknowledge that you understand their viewpoint. Avoid arguing.)

- Make it clear what role you want them to have in your marriage, now that you are one with your spouse.

6. **Troubleshoot** *(in the event that your parents go ballistic!).* If your parents are so controlling that even a diplomatic exploration of the problem results in an explosive confrontation, you must repeat that your goal was to establish your God-given marital independence, while maintaining honor for your parents and including them in your life. Even so, if this cannot be accomplished at this time, you must still, at God's instruction, claim your independence and wait

prayerfully and patiently for your parents to understand and adjust to a new and healthy relationship pattern.

Most of the time, these discussions are well received by parents and in-laws, and lead to better interactions. Even if they don't, your best shot at a happy marriage will be achieved when you "leave and cleave." Furthermore, if you don't, you are undoubtedly headed for disaster—at worst, for divorce.

Well, there you have it. A plan of action. Sound reasonable? Let's face it: Sitting down to straighten out your parents can seem like an overwhelmingly difficult task! For a lifetime they have been the ones to straighten you out. We often find that an honest, kind letter may pave the way for what will become a loving, face-to-face discussion. The following is a letter a young husband wrote to his parents to set the scene for the future discussion which would ultimately begin the healing process:

Dear Mom and Dad:

I want to begin my letter thanking you for all of the positive characteristics I see in my own life because you were there. The times that you nursed me through illness, helped me with my homework, wiped away my tears, demonstrated integrity, became my own personal cheerleaders... will always stand as monuments to the love I so definitely feel from you day to day.

With that in mind, I come to you today asking for your help. The help I am asking for is to support me in taking the next step that will truly introduce me to full adulthood. This step would strengthen my confidence and help me to know that the work you put into me has now been finished... and has been finished well.

I must be honest with you and tell you that there are times when I feel that having an opinion differing from yours could cause a breach in our relationship. I want to enjoy the freedom of voicing personal opinions when we talk, just as you do.

Even when it doesn't match yours. Even when yours is right.

Speaking of personal opinions, I am making one of the most important decisions of my life. I want to tell you that I will be marrying Ashley. Although you have expressed deep concerns that Ashley is not the woman for me, I love her with all my heart. It is fully my intention to spend the rest of my life with her. I would love your complete support. Please understand that I am willing to proceed without it. Without your support I will be missing something indescribably valuable to me. And I want you to know that.

Since the first Christmas musical at Lincoln Elementary School, I have looked out at the crowd to gain eye-contact with your approving expressions. It was always there. When I was quarterback at Muir High, I looked into the stands for approval, and it was there. When I threw my cap high into the air at graduation, I looked into the crowd, and your faces radiated the approval that has always been there.

As I take this step toward manhood and independence, I want you to know that it results from the strength you unselfishly gave to me throughout my lifetime. I have always been your son and always will be.

The time has come for a new dimension to be added to our relationship. By that I am only trying to convey that we are independent, yet supportive, of each other's journeys as adults.

This letter will be followed up by a visit soon, to assure you of my respect and love, and to clarify the boundaries I hope to establish regarding my relationship with Ashley.

With love as always,
Kevin

Our goal in writing this chapter was to lead you into the harmonious order that will preserve and promote not only your marriage, but your all-important family relationships. We believe that God intended us to cherish our mate, esteem our parents, value our friends, and learn from our adversaries.

Lest you be tempted to read this chapter and believe that we see parents as predators, be assured this is not the case. Rather, we see serious trouble in store when the priority relationship of marriage is not placed in its rightful position as God instructed.

We want to underscore that the marriage relationship is the most important human relationship. The parent-child relationship is the next most important, followed by the extended family and then friendships, associates, acquaintances, community, and even adversaries.

Couples who claim their God-given independence can successfully incorporate fulfilling relationships with parents and with in-laws, and with the valuable extended family and friendship relationships that enrich life. We hope you are encouraged by the specific information in this chapter that can help you reorder and rebuild these relationships to promote growth and pleasure in your family contacts.

THIRTEEN

~

Unwanted Surprises:
Sexual Dysfunction and
Sexual Deception

"Designed for pleasure," you say? Sex? Some couples' expectations are far greater than what they experience in their sexual relationship. For those who are frustrated and disappointed, talk of the joys of intimacy in marriage only disappoints and confuses. What is the secret of others' success? they ask. Why do we have hassles and heartbreaks in the bedroom? In rare cases the unwanted surprise in the sexual relationship is much more serious: aberrant sexual behavior.

While we realize there are some exceptions, the majority of couples can reach a satisfying, intimate physical life together. God designed us to enjoy a oneness of mind, body, and spirit with our mate. Anything that would hinder you from experiencing a fullness in your sexual relationship is worth addressing and working to overcome. (Again, we know there are a few exceptions to this possibility, and we wish to be sensitive to that. Some impairments and illnesses preclude sexual intimacy. If that is your situation, we hope you will exercise whatever forms of physical intimacy remain within your sphere.)

OVERCOMING BARRIERS TO THE JOY OF INTIMACY

You and your mate will develop a repertoire of sexual experiences over the course of your relationship. You may begin expanding that repertoire right now. As you proceed through this chapter, you may be able to identify some barriers that have kept you and your partner from experiencing the sexual intimacy you both desire. If so, we hope you will gain insight for dealing with these obstacles. Others of you may use this chapter as a road map for staying on course.

In recent decades scientific pioneering work has lifted the fog around sex and sexuality. Among the many we have to thank are Alfred C. Kinsey, and the research team of William Masters and Virginia Johnson, whose dedicated medical work has uncovered many mysteries of our sexuality. These physicians' long-standing expertise in the study of sexuality have shed light on many important factors. The role of the brain, biological and structural makeup, the role of hormones, and the differing characteristics of the male and female sexual responses have been among the factors illuminated.

Psychologists, physicians, and psychiatrists have built a significant body of information about human sexuality. Some of them view the sexual relationship from the vantage point of learned behavior and modeling: what we observed in our homes; the sexual attitudes and practices of our generation; what we have read; what was rewarded and what was punished while we were growing up—all impact the uniqueness of our sexual attitudes.

Others have a psychosocial focus: How we interact with others generally, in terms of trust and the ability to be intimate, open, and communicative, will be reflected in the sexual relationship.

Many factors make up the experience of a couple's sexual practices and experiences, and understanding these factors and responses can greatly enhance a marriage. Sexuality is a changing experience, and you have a lifetime to unfold the mysteries of your relationship in the bedroom.

To begin, we wish to review two models of sexuality. The first, called the *linear model*, moves from stimulation to climax.

A ─────────────> B
stimulation   climax

This model reflects the practice of many couples. It begins with sexual foreplay, followed by intercourse. If the partner reaches climax, it is considered "good sex" or "good lovemaking." If not, feelings of disappointment and inadequacy often emerge in both partners. More selfish mates base the success of their lovemaking on whether or not they themselves reach climax, with little concern for their partner's experience. For many, the linear model also creates performance anxiety. Both partners may feel pressured to reach climax not only for pleasure, but to protect each other from frustration and feelings of inadequacy.

We believe this model promotes a distorted view of lovemaking. Those who follow this model are likely to be disappointed every time they make love and one of the partners is fatigued, not well, or has a reduced sex drive. This model leads to boredom and routine. It's an all-or-nothing approach. It's either all good or all bad. This model is unimaginative. The couples who take this approach often have not considered that other more fulfilling options exist. We want to introduce you to a richer and fuller model of sexual relating—a model that promotes acceptance, pleasure, variety, and dignity.

This second model, called the *pleasuring model,* consists of a circle with many points. Each point on the circle adds unique value and personality to your sexual pleasure. Each phase works to embellish the previous and following phases.

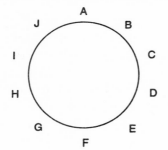

Couples who practice this full-orchestra lovemaking are sure to develop an appreciation for the entire symphony! The pleasuring model emphasizes that each experience within the sexual encounter is offered for the pleasure of the partner. Each encounter is offered to awaken erotic, sensual feelings in the mate. While this model includes stimulation and climax just like the linear model, it also incorporates many intimate exchanges along the way. Here is a list of examples:

- Emotional connection (intimate talking and whispers)

- Cleanliness (taking a shower together or washing the other's back while bathing)

- Anticipation through invitation

- Verbal foreplay

- Affectionate touch; massage and caressing; holding

- Sexual foreplay

- Sexual intercourse

- Climax

- Afterglow

- Sleep

The pleasuring model focuses both partners on giving and receiving, on pleasuring and being pleasured. Each experience along the way is valued. In the process, a considerable level of affection, love, passion, and emotional connection are exchanged. Whether or not climax is reached will undoubtedly be a consideration. However, the lovemaking will not be evaluated on the basis of climax. This is an exchange of love. It is a deep physical, emotional, and spiritual encounter.

COMMON DYSFUNCTIONS

What are the most common kinds of sexual dysfunction? A prominent sex therapist, Helen Singer Kaplan, concludes that there are six major symptoms of sexual dysfunction—three among men and three among women. For men the symptoms are: difficulty achieving erection; premature ejaculation; and having a problem ejaculating. For women the symptoms are: general sexual dysfunction; orgastic dysfunction; and vaginismus.

We will define each of these symptoms in everyday terms. The greater a couple's understanding of these, the less mystery there will be. We want to assure you that there are explanations and solutions available for each of these problems. When addressed openly, steps can be taken to bring sexual fulfillment into a previously unfulfilling relationship.

The following is a short glossary of terms related to male and female sexual difficulties:

Erectile dysfunction: He cannot achieve an erection or cannot maintain the erection during intercourse.

Premature ejaculation: After just a few thrusts, he ejaculates. This may occur in each sexual attempt, or may occur randomly in relation to performance pressure and anxiety.

Retarded ejaculation: He is unable to ejaculate, although he has no problem with erection before and during intercourse (stimulation is adequate and the desire to ejaculate is present).

General sexual dysfunction (frigidity): She has little or no sexual pleasure when stimulated. She receives gratification only from the closeness and touch.

Orgastic dysfunction: She is unable to achieve orgasm, even though she is sexually responsive otherwise. (Some women experience both general sexual dysfunction and orgastic dysfunction. Remember the two phases; they don't respond physiologically to the excitement stage, nor do they reach climax. These are separate functions. They can occur together or alone.)

Vaginismus: The vaginal canal (introitus) is surrounded by muscles. In vaginismus, these muscles spasm when penetration is attempted, thus limiting penetration. She may fear penetration (phobic avoidance) and also experience general sexual dysfunction (no pleasure from stimulation.) Or, she may experience pleasure in all aspects except penetration. This problem may or may not be due to abnormal anatomy. A pelvic exam can differentiate which problem exists. Appropriate treatment can then be given to alleviate either a physical problem or a psychological reaction.

If you see any of these male or female sexual problems in your marriage, there are a number of factors that could be contributing to the difficulties. In the next section, you can explore some of the possible reasons for the problems. You will learn that sometimes the contributing factors are not even physical. Other times they are, and help is available.

HOW CAN WE ASSESS IT?

You and your mate can respond to the following list of factors. They are categorized under several headings, each of which contributes to the overall sexual experience. Check the items that concern you or your mate.

Physical factors:

___ A health problem that affects your ability or interest in sex in your marriage

___ Use of drugs or alcohol

___ Contraceptives that you disagree about, or that cause undue side effects

___ Infections

___ Use of prescribed drugs that seem to be reducing ability or desire

___ History of rape or sexual abuse

___ Physical fatigue due to stress

Environmental factors:

___ Lack of privacy

___ Poor timing

___ Lack of adequate time (too rushed, pressured)

___ Uncomfortable setting (bad mattress, cluttered or unclean surroundings)

Current stresses:

___ Loss of job

___ Severe financial stress

___ Death of a loved one

___ Sleep disorders

___ Tension in the marriage

___ Severe illness in child or mate

___ Other _____

Relationship factors:

___ Unresolved conflicts

___ Hostility

___ Poor communication

___ Avoidance
___ Lack of time together
___ Overinvolvement in other interests or with other people
___ Lack of desire on the part of one or the other partner

Sexual problems:
___ Lack of initiating
___ Lack of adequate emotional connection and foreplay
   (atmosphere, timing, setting, caressing and affection,
   talking)
___ Inability to get excited (for her, no excitement and lubri-
   cation; for him, no excitement and erection)
___ Painful penetration for her, often leading each to give up
   or feel inadequate
___ Erection problem
___ She doesn't reach orgasm
___ He doesn't reach orgasm
___ He prematurely ejaculates
___ He has difficulty ejaculating
___ The resolution stage lacks connectedness (The couple
   doesn't linger, hold each other, or interact during this
   stage. There is an abrupt ending to the sexual encoun-
   ters.)

HOW CAN WE FIND HELP?

The checklist above will be helpful in identifying the factors
that might be contributing to any problems in your sexual relationship. If you have concerns in any of the areas mentioned,
we recommend the following options:

1. *If the problems appear to be physical,* consult your physician
   to determine more specifically the cause and the appropriate
   solutions. To gain the best assessment, be specific and
   detailed in your description of the problem.

2. *If the problems seem to be mainly relational,* seek guidance through appropriate reading, meet with your pastor, or consult a therapist. From there you should be able to decide on an appropriate course of action.

3. *If the problems are mostly sexual in nature,* they may actually involve all of the above concerns. It would be worthwhile to read more about sexual matters (see the "Sexuality" division under "Recommended Reading" at the end of this book). In addition, it would be advisable to consult a physician or therapist. They can assist you in determining the severity of the problem, and can recommend appropriate solutions through either treatment or referral.

Sometimes, it is a matter of gaining more understanding about sexual matters. Other times, more intensive help is needed. A professional can relieve stress and confusion, as well as offer direction and assistance.

Sex therapy is recommended only when both partners want to develop a more satisfying sexual relationship. If there is hostility between the partners, it is necessary to treat the anger and hostility first. Once the anger and hostility are resolved, the partners will be able to create the safe and accepting emotional atmosphere essential to the effectiveness of sex therapy.

In past generations, couples did not discuss sexual matters very well. Instead, they usually learned to live with the pain and frustrations, or avoided their sexual relationship. We are living today in a marvelous time of opportunity for couples of any age to be free from the closed-mindedness, shame, and ignorance that marred so many sexual relationships in marriages in the past. You have the opportunity to learn, overcome, and develop a mutually fulfilling sexual relationship in your marriage. It is a beautiful process to witness a couple overcoming the obstacles that keep them from experiencing the fullness of the expression of love in their sexual relationship. They discover how to drop their guard, communicate gently, and exchange the tenderness they always had for each other. It is our hope that you will seek the help and resources that can bring a richness to the physical relationship so splendidly designed by God for your marriage.

FACING ABERRANT SEXUAL BEHAVIOR IN MARRIAGE

Most couples enter marriage assuming that most things of substance have been voluntarily disclosed to them by their mate. It comes as quite a shock when they learn that this has not happened.

That was certainly Rachel's assumption when she married Bjorn. Her husband was the epitome of the health-conscious male. He paid enormous attention to his physical needs—nutrition, physical fitness, a glowing tan. Appearance was paramount with him. Bjorn was very conscious of his clothing and wouldn't be caught dead with a single hair out of place.

Rachel never needed to worry about Bjorn's appearance, and she was exceptionally attractive as well, seemingly without effort. Many of their friends joked about the possibility that they fell off the top of a wedding cake to begin their life together!

A month after their fifth anniversary, Rachel was to discover the unimaginable. It was a little after 2:00 A.M. She wasn't sure what awakened her. There was enough light from the full moon to reveal that Bjorn was not in bed. Concerned, Rachel got up to see if he was okay. As she entered the hallway, she could see the flickering light of the television creating lines and shadows on the family room wall. She assumed Bjorn was watching television because he could not sleep. She walked into the family room so quietly that Bjorn had no knowledge of her presence. Rachel was shocked and confused by what her eyes beheld: Bjorn was lying in front of the television, dressed in *Rachel's* most provocative lingerie!

Rachel hoped this was a bad dream—because it was far too bizarre to be real. She had to pinch herself to see if she was awake.

This was no dream. Rachel switched on the family room light, and Bjorn sat up in horror. Their eyes met for only a second. Then Bjorn looked at the floor in shame and humiliation. Rachel gasped, "Bjorn, what do you think you are doing?" He retreated to the couch and turned his posture away from her.

"I guess you had to find out someday. I just couldn't bring myself to tell you!"

Rachel stared at Bjorn and said, "Tell me what?"

"You're not going to like this, Rachel."

"I'm not liking it already. Tell me *what*!" she demanded.

"I haven't been completely honest with you. Since I was twelve years old, I have felt as if I were a woman locked in a man's body. I suppose if I had been honest with myself, I could have had an operation so that my inner feelings would match my body. But, other people's feelings about that kind of thing kept me from pursuing that possibility. So, I did the next best thing. I was attracted to you, not as a man is attracted to a woman, but as a *woman* is attracted to a woman. I don't know if this makes sense to you, but for the last five years I have been living out a lesbian fantasy with you. You're everything I ever hoped for in a woman! I hope you understand. It is so hard to tell you this. I can imagine what you are thinking."

Rachel fell against the family room wall, as her knees buckled beneath her. She felt as if she was losing consciousness. She breathed deeply several times before saying, "Understand! Understand! You've just told me that you're living as a woman in a man's body? You call our marriage a lesbian fantasy, and you're asking if I understand? No, I don't understand. Not at all! I married you thinking you were in love with me... a man, in love with me, a woman! You have lied. Have you ever lied! You have made a mockery of this marriage! How could you justify keeping this from me?"

"You were happy when you didn't know, weren't you? Everything was working out okay. That's why I didn't tell you," he said. He inquired with complete sincerity, "Has it ever occurred to you that you might be a lesbian? I've thought that all along."

Rachel moved a step closer to rage. "First of all, Bjorn, get my lingerie off your sleazy body. Then throw it in the trash! You make me sick!"

A wave of nausea passed over her and she ran for the bathroom. As quickly as she could manage, she pulled on some clothes and jammed some personal items into an overnight bag. Within minutes, she was slamming the front door behind her. Not knowing what to do or whom to talk to, she went to a twenty-four-hour coffee shop to collect her thoughts. She decided she needed to see her pastor and was at the doorstep of his office when he arrived that morning. Before she knew it, she was crying uncontrollably, attempting all the while to choke out the horrible revelations of the night before. She was finally able to get the words out.

The pastor listened with compassion and understanding. These were difficult words to hear; more difficult still for Rachel to face. Somewhat bewildered at first, the pastor began to counsel her. He said, "This is clearly a form of adultery and homosexuality. Your husband made your marriage a charade from the beginning. You have every right to step out of it. I am confident that if you had known this earlier, you would have sought an annulment. There would have been more than adequate grounds. A divorce is appropriate under the circumstances."

The pastor did not understand why Bjorn had chosen this lifestyle. He could only speculate what could cause a man such confusion about his sexual identity. But he was certain that Rachel should not be required to continue in a marriage built on a lie.

Rachel made an unequivocal decision for an immediate

divorce. Then, following the divorce, she was tormented by self-doubt. Bjorn's question to her about her own sexual identity echoed in her mind. How could she have chosen him? He wasn't doing anything unnatural with her. Or was he? How could he have deceived her so completely? To explore these doubts and fears, she sought personal counseling. In time, she was given full assurance that she was simply a woman who had been deceived—nothing more, nothing less.

During the weeks that followed, other evidence of Bjorn's dark and secret life emerged. While packing personal items, Rachel uncovered a box filled with homosexual pornography and a collection of adult videos. She had never seen these before. She was also revolted to find a stack of perfumed letters, tied with a satin ribbon, addressed to Bjorn by a man who called himself Jackie. It was discovered during the divorce action that Bjorn had rented a separate apartment, where he kept thousands of dollars worth of women's apparel and cosmetics. Bjorn had indulged in his lifestyle for many years. He even belonged to a club made up of men with his sexual orientation. It was abundantly clear that Bjorn had no intention of ever turning away from his lifestyle.

* * *

This account illustrates the pain and destruction thrust upon a marriage by aberrant sexual behavior. Hidden sexual practices such as homosexuality, bisexuality, cross-dressing, and fascination with pornography are far more common among married individuals than one might think. These are men and women who deceive their mates and hide their true sexual practices and preferences behind a wall of lies. When their secrets are revealed, the marriage disintegrates. Typically, the mate is left to heal from tremendous pain, confusion, and self-doubt.

This kind of sin is not simply a matter of one's lifestyle preference. At its heart, it is adultery. It adulterates the holy purpose for which God created marital sexuality. The biblical Greek word for sin, *hamartano*, is an archery term, meaning "to miss the mark." *Sin is a violation of God's intention—it misses the mark of his will for our lives.*

Where there is aberrant sexual behavior, there is little hope of transformation of that behavior. Once established as a lifestyle, few seem to seek a way back. Even among those who seek help for reorientation, the success rate is dismal. If you find yourself married to someone who is practicing aberrant sexual behavior, you will have some hard decisions to make.

As counselors, we would be irresponsible to offer you much hope for your marital relationship. We do, however, believe that our God can help you recover and get back *the years the locusts have eaten* (Joel 2:25). As for the bisexual partner, or the partner indulging in a variety of sexual sins, there is only one hope and solution: get help. There are support groups in abundance where you will find understanding, guidance, and support for recovery.

∽

FOURTEEN

Echoes from Eden:
Family of Origin Issues

M arriage always brings together an individual male from one family culture and an individual female from another family culture. This is the makings of culture shock! The expectations each partner brings into the marriage will make sense to that partner but may seem completely foreign to the mate. It's as though a foreign language were being spoken in each person's home. When you come together as partners, you are still speaking your native language. Sometimes a translation is needed.

To complicate things further, you bring into marriage baggage from your childhood experiences. It is important to be sensitive to each other's family culture and family history. The more you learn about each other, the more sensitive you can be to upholding the important "cultural" values and special needs in your partner that arise from his or her past. Let's explore your family culture, and that of your spouse.

If you could choose your family of origin—your mom, dad, and siblings—would you choose the family God ordained for you?

If you answered yes, circle the letters of following responses which apply to you (if you answered no, you may either read through these statements or proceed to the next list of statements):

a. *You learned a great deal growing up in your family,* and you wouldn't trade the benefit of that learning for anything.

b. *You cherish your family relationships,* recognizing and accepting the imperfections.

c. *You have overcome a great deal of pain from growing up* and now accept your family as is, strengths and weaknesses.

d. *You grew up in a healthy environment* where adults and children were loved and respected, and conflicts were resolved relatively well. You would happily choose the same family, and you have a smile on your face just thinking about it.

Many people have come to accept and enjoy aspects of their childhood and the adult relationships they now have with their parents and siblings, with the lively and diverse addition of in-laws and children. To the extent that you do, we consider you blessed. For some this has always been the case; for others this newfound comfort has come after much pain, processing of emotions and experiences, and consistent spiritual development. For still others, the pain you endured in childhood still echoes in the present.

If you answered that you wished you *had grown up in another family,* circle any of the following responses which describe why:

a. *You resent the abuses* that occurred in your home and would give anything to have an adult life free of those scars. You secretly wish you had grown up in another family.

b. *Your family was entirely too restrictive and rigid.* You could never attain to its high standards; nothing you did seemed to be good enough.

c. **You still experience life with fear.** Fear was taught in your home through intimidation and over-control. You now view the world as an unsafe place.

d. **You learned not to trust.** Your parents didn't trust each other, they didn't trust outsiders, and they didn't trust you. Now you trust no one.

e. **You fear intimacy.** In your home, no one was allowed to be close to another. Things such as expression of feelings, appropriate touch and affection, and affirmation and approval were strictly off-limits. Even now, you rarely offer these things to the people you care most about, and you feel very uncomfortable around those who *are* able to feel, show affection, affirm, and compliment.

If your marriage is being severely affected by some unresolved issues from your past, you may wonder: What brought me to this point? Why am I here? When did I arrive here? Where am I going? Who will get me out?

Our family of origin makes a profound impact on our life. Over a span of eighteen to twenty-four years, we absorb, mimic, and enhance the images and actions modeled by our parents and extended families. It is here that we obtain our values for good or for evil. We learn to be responsible or irresponsible. In watching our parents, grandparents, aunts and uncles, we learn how men relate to women and how women relate to men. We understand the value or lack of value of money. We decide what is natural and what is unnatural. We decide what is sinful and what is righteous. We gain the foundation for our political viewpoints and work ethic. We learn humor, or a lack of humor. We learn to appreciate and value others.

Do you enjoy and embrace people of other religions, cultures, and backgrounds? If so, you probably have your family to thank. Do you fear or hate people different than yourself? You can probably "credit" your family for that as well.

We cannot overestimate the influence of our family of origin. The truth is, we may come to realize that they were a good example or a bad example, or a combination of the two. Where they have served as a good example, we can emulate those strengths. Every experience is valuable—even if only to serve as a bad example.

Family influence is passed from generation to generation. The Bible recognizes and underscores the importance of this principle when it says, "The Lord is slow to anger, abounding in love and forgiving sin and rebellion. Yet he does not leave the guilty unpunished; he punishes the children for the sin of the fathers to the third and the fourth generation" (Numbers 14:18). The sad truth is, families that live abusive, addictive lifestyles can count on their children learning their ways. Further, their children's children will bear the scars, showing similar behaviors toward their own children. There is hope, however. We can break the chain in our own generation. The good news of the Numbers passage is that we can break away from the negative influences of our family of origin if we choose to break the cycle.

Family of origin issues encompass many subjects from abuse to addictions of many kinds. It is our purpose to introduce these issues because of their effect on the marriage. It is beyond the scope of this book to give adequate coverage to each of these issues, but we encourage you to address this matter as you work to break the cycle of unfinished business. Certainly the journey itself involves an intensive healing process, often including therapy, support group involvement, prayer, and reading. For that journey, we recommend outside help. It is our goal to offer guidelines for couples to support each other in the process of healing from past pain. As you continue reading this chapter, you will witness three couples' behaviors in the face of unfinished family of origin issues. Did they face the problems and work together toward resolution or did they pretend the problems would go away by themselves?

FAMILY PORTRAITS

Let us introduce you to three couples. As you read, you will see how each partner worked to overcome his or her "unfinished business" from their family of origin, and improved their marriage in the process.

Coming of age. Darren and Sarah walked into a counselor's office for premarital counseling. Their eyes spoke of tension and depression. What should have been the happiest time of their lives was not. Their unhappiness was clear to the counselor even before they spoke.

They had come in to hear the results of their written premarital test. Some of the results indicated problems. Darren came from an unusual home. Both of his parents were described on the test as extremely controlling people. That interested the counselor, and he asked Darren who was the most controlling of the two.

Darren looked at Sarah to make sure he answered correctly. With a halting voice, he answered, "I think, my father." Sarah nodded approvingly, without smiling, as if the mentioning of his father was uncomfortable for her. "Is that important?" Darren asked.

"Yes, it is, Darren," the counselor replied. "You have scored at the extreme end of the scale, revealing yourself to be a highly submissive person. Sarah, on the other hand, has scored in the middle of the ideal realm of this scale, depicting a responsible and reliable person. It makes me wonder how you perceive Sarah after two years of relationship. My guess is that at times you perceive Sarah to be very bossy. Also, I would imagine you often feel unsure of your manhood while in her presence."

Sarah's head dropped to the table as she whispered, "You got that right!" She sat up, looked at the counselor, and said, "He says I'm too pushy all the time, especially after he's asked me to make important decisions—ones that really *he* should have made in the first place. But, he gets all nervous when he has to make a decision. Sometimes, he gets into a major crisis over whether or not to get french fries with his burger. Then I say, 'Get them if you want them.' He says, 'Do you think I should?' I say, 'Darren, make a choice. I don't care. Just hurry up. If it will help things along, just get 'em!' Then he gets them, but he becomes pouty and moody over the decision. He silently blames me."

"Darren," the counselor said, "tell me something. Were you allowed to make personal decisions growing up?" Sarah shook her head no before Darren answered, "I don't think so."

"When did you make your first decision as an adult?"

Searching his mind, Darren expressed, "Well, I'm not sure when I made my first choice. But I remember that when I was in the Marines, I called my father for permission to go out with the guys. I was twenty-four years old at the time. He let me go."

"Darren, do you still ask your dad for permission?"

"Maybe, sometimes," he replied ashamedly.

Sarah rolled her eyes. With crossed arms and pursed lips, she spoke with a tinge of anger. "More than sometimes. He goes to his parents for everything. I don't get it."

"Well, Sarah," the counselor went on, "maybe I can explain it to you. This test seems to indicate that Darren has never been allowed to make decisions. In fact, I would say that one of the things that attracted Darren to you was your confidence in decision making. If he could count on you to make decisions, it would keep him out of a danger zone of sorts. You remove the risk he feels. He can make decisions; he's just not used to it.

"This is what we call a family of origin issue. As it stands, Darren is caught in the middle of wanting to be a man, but not feeling he has the permission to claim his manhood. In essence, he performed as a track star, but his parents did not pass the baton during the relay. I have a feeling that Darren's hand is reaching for the baton as we speak. Darren and Sarah, I want to assure you that this is not a rare problem. Also, I am happy to tell you that it is one of the easier problems to solve."

* * *

The preceding story illustrates how many of us may have gotten stuck in the past. Sometimes the circumstances of life give us the opportunity to grow up. Sometimes we grow because someone extends a hand to us. Sadly, there are occasions where people don't grow up. For the most part, that is only because they refuse to take the baton and run with it.

If you find yourself in a similar situation, you might be helped by how Sarah and Darren worked together to build his confidence and decision making skills:

1. *Even though Sarah was responsible and took initiative, she agreed to defer to Darren all joint decisions that had to be made for a week.* They would meet with the counselor the next week and assess how things went. The goal was to give more and more of the responsibility to Darren. It was important that Sarah be patient with Darren, allowing him to take the time he needed, and most importantly, refusing to make the decision for him. Her cooperation in not compensating for him was key to his ability to grow in this area. The counselor told her, "As Darren gains more practice, you will feel less like a mother and more like a partner with him."

2. *Darren agreed to try not to think of Sarah as pushy or overbearing.* He realized that he would not always feel comfortable making decisions—especially at first. But he agreed to keep trying. It wasn't automatic; sometimes a decision didn't get made and they suffered the consequences; but over time Darren felt more confident. He realized he had to

take the baton from Sarah if he was going to be a full partner in the marriage.

3. *Finally, Darren and Sarah agreed to see a counselor together
on a weekly basis,* to get insight and support for working
through this important area in their relationship.

Abuse: trust betrayed. Teresa needed someone to talk to.
Somebody she could trust. She felt like she was going crazy.
The one person she knew she could rely on was her sister-in-
law, Rhonda. They had become very close during the nine
years she had been married to Rhonda's brother, Ted. They
were to meet at Shoney's in Albuquerque for lunch. Each
would drive nearly forty miles to meet and talk. Rhonda sensed
a note of desperation in Teresa's voice, and would not have
considered for a second missing an opportunity to reach out to
her.

Rhonda knew her brother was growing increasingly frustrated in the marriage, and didn't have a clue what he should do
to improve the relationship. Maybe, by talking with Teresa, she
could gain some helpful insights into her brother's situation.

Teresa and Rhonda pulled into Shoney's at exactly the same
time, parking side by side. Teresa hugged Rhonda extra tightly
when they embraced. They were well into their meal when
Teresa started crying. Rhonda reached across the table and
held her hand, saying, "We'll work this out."

Teresa blubbered, "What if I don't even know what is
wrong?"

"Then we'll find out together," Rhonda reassured. "I know
that things are difficult between you and Ted. Tell me about it,
Teresa."

"It's really hard, Rhonda. I love your brother. I couldn't ask
for a better husband. He's been really understanding during
these past months. But something's happened to me. I haven't
been myself. Everything's fine until Ted wants to make love.

When he approaches me, I get this feeling that I can't breathe; I want to run. Suddenly, I don't trust him. And, Rhonda, he's never done anything to hurt me. There's something wrong with *me*. And I don't know what it is! You've gotta help me. You're the only one I can trust with this."

Rhonda was a registered nurse who worked for a gynecologist and had seen similar reactions in women they treated. Trusting her experience and intuition, she asked gently, "Teresa, who hurt you when you were young? Who was it that made you feel so frightened and ashamed?"

Teresa looked shocked. She had never discussed this dark moment in her life with anyone. She wondered how Rhonda could possibly have zeroed in so quickly. "I, I don't know where to begin... uh, I..."

Rhonda, sensing she had opened a Pandora's box in a setting with insufficient privacy, motioned to the waitress for the bill. She said, "Let's go someplace where it's safe to talk. I know just the place."

Returning to the parking lot, Rhonda invited Teresa to ride with her to a beautiful park she had noticed on the way to Shoney's. Rhonda held Teresa's hand and invited, "Go ahead. What were you starting to say at the restaurant?"

Before she could speak, Teresa fell into Rhonda's arms and wept. She said, "I feel so ashamed. I feel so dirty. This would hurt Ted if he knew. So, promise me you won't tell him."

"I promise," whispered Rhonda.

"I have a secret. It started on my eleventh birthday. I had a really fun birthday party. My mom drove my friends home and I stayed home alone with my uncle. He asked me to sit on his lap. I remember he called me Sugarcake. He asked me if I remembered how we used to play horsey when I was a little girl. I told him I did. And he asked me if it was fun. And I told him it was. Then he began to bounce me like I was a little girl. And... and... and..." Teresa again collapsed in Rhonda's arms, crying like a little girl. "It didn't stop there, Rhonda. I let him touch me and he made me touch him. I can't tell you the rest."

Rhonda held her sister-in-law and spoke softly. "Teresa, it's gonna be okay. No wonder you have been suffering. I'm sure my brother will be understanding. He will want to help you work through this. I am so thankful we could be together today. I love you like my own sister."

After a long conversation, Teresa asked Rhonda if she would be willing to call Ted and let him know what had happened. Rhonda agreed and they found a private phone booth. The two of them exchanged the phone as they each revealed the source of the pain to Ted. Ted was every bit as supportive as Rhonda had expected.

* * *

How did Teresa and Ted work through this issue?

1. *They met with a professional counselor from their church who specialized in helping survivors of molestation.*

2. *Teresa attended a number of individual counseling sessions.* In addition, she attended a support group for women who had been molested. With the insights from the counselor and other survivors, she learned that her trust in an adult had been betrayed. Over time she was able to separate the incident from her identity. She realized she was innocent, and that her uncle was fully responsible for the betrayal and trauma he had caused.

3. *She and Ted received counseling together on occasion, in addition to her individual sessions.* They learned that Teresa was mentally reliving the molestation in their marriage. The echoes of the past were drowning out the clear, beautiful tones of the present. As they worked through the many

issues with the counselor, they were able to overcome the pain.

4. Teresa committed herself to face her pain and work through it. And Ted committed himself to learning about the process and becoming an informed supporter of his wife. The echoes eventually faded into the distance. From time to time, an echo from the past is heard and they talk it through until it silences.

If you were sexually abused as a child and have not received professional help, chances are that your marriage is being affected in a negative way. If so, we encourage you to take the same steps that Teresa and Ted took.

Expression of love. Sharon had been disappointed in her marriage for years. For her, walking down the aisle was simply the continuation of what had been an extremely romantic journey, but that was not the case for Jim. For him, marriage marked a conquest. It was the culmination, not a continuation, of the journey. Shared time, deep affection, and romantic settings were all part of the courtship ritual. And he had played his role well. But Jim had come from a family that displayed marriage not as a continuation of courtship but as a bland, business-as-usual exercise. It was a "there's a place for everything, and everything in its place" type of existence.

Sharon's parents were in their late fifties, and were more in love, by their own admission, than ever before. Theirs was a marriage that improved with age like a good wine. Many of their friends were amused by the freedom of expression in their marriage. One friend said, "Look at Charlie. He can hardly keep his hands off Rose!" They were wonderful caretakers. It was hard to say whether she was his only need or he was her only need. Sharon wanted the kind of marriage her parents had.

If the first year of Sharon and Jim's marriage was any indication, it wasn't going to happen. Sharon was a woman who
faced things head-on. She shared both her commitment and
her disappointment with Jim. "I'm just not happy. Marriage
isn't what I thought it would be."

Jim was dumbfounded. He had no idea that he was not
happily married. As Jim grew up, he observed absolutely no
affection expressed between his mother and father. His mother
was severely addicted to alcohol and prescription drugs. He
remembered thinking many times during childhood,
"Mother's eyes were open, but nobody was home." Not only
was no affection shown between his parents, it wasn't shown
to him either. His parents were like empty wells. It was necessary to talk to keep food in the house, the bills paid, and to
know where people were going and when they would be
home. What you thought or felt about anything just didn't get
talked about. It was an unwritten rule. No one listened. No
one asked. No one was interested. For all intents and purposes,
his mother was one of the children. It was strange, but Jim
couldn't imagine his parents having a sexual relationship.
There were three children to prove that something must have
happened. But the nature of their day-to-day relationship made
the thought of sexual intimacy seem foreign.

Jim truly loved Sharon with all of his heart. It's just that his
heart was unskilled and uneducated in the art of love. Often,
the skills of love are transferred from parents to children in a
natural, day-to-day demonstration of affection. Jim had never
seen it. He hadn't felt it. How was he to duplicate it?

Jim was humble. He asked Sharon to help him understand
what he needed to do to make her happy. Sharon thought a
moment and replied, "If you treated me now like you treated
me before our wedding, that would make me happy." Jim
asked honestly, "How have I changed?" Sharon smiled, seeing
Jim's sincerity. "Honey, I can't remember you watching TV for
one hour during our courtship. And now I can't tear you away

from the screen." Jim had a flashback, picturing his father slumped on the couch in front of the television, watching anything and everything that came on. Jim knew he had fallen into the same pattern.

He also realized that he had made it difficult for Sharon to talk to him because he even insisted on watching the commercials. "Sharon, I'm acting like my dad. He watched TV for hours too. And he didn't have a very good marriage either. TV watching didn't help matters. It just dawned on me—I think I know how to be a good person; but I don't know how to be a good husband. I can tell you this, though. There isn't anything in this life that I want more than to make you happy. If the first step is kickin' in this screen, I'll do it right now!"

Sharon tackled Jim around the neck and affectionately kissed him on the cheek. "I like the direction you are heading. But, I think we can get there without breaking the TV."

"How?" Jim asked.

Sharon considered his question thoughtfully. "Could we talk for an hour when you get home from work? Like, maybe while you get cleaned up? I want you to know what happens to me each day. And I want to know what happens in your day, too. Would you be embarrassed to hold my hand in public, like at the mall or the show? Would you put your arm around me while we're watching TV? I would really love it if you did. It meant so much to me when you used to do those things!"

Jim asked, "Do we need to go to a marriage counselor?"

"If you keep talking like you're talking now, I believe you and I can do it alone. But, if we can't, I'm willing to do whatever it takes. I love you, Jim. I want to grow old with you!"

In jest, she added, "When I walked down the aisle with you, it was 'till death do us part.' Jim, I meant that. I just don't want to die of boredom!"

* * *

Jim and Sharon represent literally hundreds of thousands of couples who are mildly handicapped by the pain of their family of origin issues. The cure for the ills of couples like Jim and Sharon comes from a true desire to love their partner. Most of the solutions to these problems can be found when we ask our mates what they need from us that they are not getting. Here are some common responses we have heard to that question; they represent important cures that will make your marriage the priority it deserves to be:

- Quality time
- Quantity time
- Affectionate touch
- Deep and honest communication
- Active listening
- Faithfulness
- Complete disclosure
- Desire to grow and learn
- Willingness to change
- Humble attitude

Family of origin issues vary greatly, but may include:

- Traumatic experiences which remain unhealed
- Poor role modeling which we must unlearn
- Voids for which we must find appropriate fulfillment, or education we never received, such as learning what "normal" is
- Unresolved emotions and inappropriate means of expression
- Communication and relationship skills

There are many excellent resource books on family of origin issues. We have included a list of them in our Recommended Reading section in the back of this book. We recommend that you seek out and read them for help in overcoming the pain, finishing the unfinished business, and "breaking the cycle" in your generation. We support your decision to learn, to read, to attend educational talks that will help you grow. We recommend pastoral and professional counseling and support groups as you seek to silence or quiet the echoes from Eden. Whatever your family culture, you can work to enhance your marriage. It is your responsibility to take charge of the predators from the past that find their way into your marriage.

FIFTEEN

The Seventh Commandment: Concerning Adultery

F ew sins are as lethal to a family and to a marriage as adultery. What seems to the adulterer an exotic adventure, a welcome diversion, is no more than a selfish vacation into self-indulgence. It introduces into the marriage a virulent, emotional virus, and it rarely stops until it drags bewildered partners into the troubling world of the divorced.

Affairs are born in darkness, they are nurtured in darkness, and they end in darkness. The participants skulk around, hiding and lying. Cheating has never been deemed a virtue. For a season, the sensual feeling adulterers enjoy mimics love. But adultery cannot be love. The Bible tells us in 1 Corinthians that "love builds up," but adultery inevitably tears down, rips up, and spits out its victims. The landscape is littered with the remains of devastated wives, disillusioned husbands, and brokenhearted children who can no longer idealize their parents as persons of substance and integrity. Only five percent of adulteries turn into remarriages and those marriages rarely last. How could they, when they have been built on foundations of sand?

WHAT DOES THE BIBLE SAY?

The adulterer gets no respect from the Bible. None at all. Read Proverbs 6:32-33: "A man who commits adultery lacks judgment; whoever does so, destroys himself. Blows and disgrace are his lot, and his shame will never be wiped away."

This verse points out several things about adulterers:

1. They "lack judgment." (Elsewhere, Scripture calls them fools.)

2. Ultimately it is *themselves* they hurt. (The Bible says the adulterer "destroys himself.")

3. They will pay a price. (Big consequences always follow adultery.)

4. They will always bear their shame. (They are forever "disgraced.")

Studies suggest that, during a ten-year marriage, as many as 65 percent of males and 55 percent of females will commit adultery. Only about 15 percent of their marriages will survive. Something to think about, isn't it? It's a high-stakes sin, and Christians are not the only ones who have noticed. Even Hollywood has warned us about the dangers of adultery—in *Fatal Attraction*, starring Glenn Close and Michael Douglas. People walked out of theaters scared straight. Following the film, there was a measurable decline in extramarital sexual activity for a time! Another movie, *Indecent Proposal*, starring Robert Redford and Demi Moore, warned us that there is no such thing as a meaningless one-night stand. Adultery is always meaningful. The effect of even a one-night stand will remain with you.

Adultery can never enjoy God's blessing. God chose to mention it in his top ten list of sins; adultery stands as number seven, right after murder, in the Ten Commandments. For whatever reason, God chose marital sex to be the most significant bonding agent between a man and a woman. Marital sex is the super glue of marriage. Adultery dissolves the bond, and destroys and fractures the marriage relationship.

When Jesus was asked about the legitimate grounds for ending a marriage, he only mentioned one thing: adultery. Just adultery. (It would be worth your while to review Matthew 19:3-9.) Because he had made us, he knew that the act of adultery would be for marriage partners nearly impossible to forgive, even if forgiveness was asked for or sought. It follows from Jesus' statement that God values faithfulness even more than he hates divorce (see Malachi 2:16).

Let's explore the anatomy of adultery. Read the following stories and see whether you may be headed in the wrong direction. If you are, we want to say, "Friend, turn around quickly. Right now. Do not hesitate!"

THE CAT AND THE CONDOM

Heather sat down across the walnut table in the counselor's office and sighed, "My marriage is in trouble. Curt is telling me he's not sure if he loves me anymore. He says he's not sure that he ever loved me. Can I be that stupid? That in five years I never noticed he didn't love me?"

"I don't think you're stupid, Heather," replied the counselor. An executive in a travel business, Heather was articulate and had a quick wit. "May I ask some questions?" the counselor continued.

"Yes, please do," Heather offered.

"How long, would you say, has Curt been different?"

"Different?"

"Emotionally distant, less talkative, anxious, troubled, those sorts of things."

"Oh! I would say about three months."

"Have there been any changes in his schedule?"

"Yes, he has been gone more. He is even working some Saturdays now."

"When did that start, Heather?" the counselor pursued.

"About three months ago."

"Has he bought some new clothes recently?" he inquired.

"How did you know that?"

"Just a guess. When did you begin to see a decline in your sexual activity? Would that be about three months ago, also?"

"Yes," she said, leaning forward. "What are you thinking?"

"Please bear with me, Heather. Let me ask one more question. When Curt is away from home, can you reach him? Could you have immediate access to him after normal working hours, say, if your little girl had an emergency?"

"Well, no, not really. He works in a high-rise and the switchboard closes down after 6:00 P.M. I wondered for a while if he was having an affair. One night I got real suspicious, then drove to his office building to see if he was there. His car was in the parking lot. But I still asked him if he was having an affair. He got angry. He said he'd tell me if he ever did have an affair. He asked me if I could ever remember when he had lied to me even once. I had to say no. Then he said, 'Even asking me if I'd committed adultery was a cheap shot.'"

"You want to know what I think, Heather?" the counselor asked rhetorically.

She nodded, "Yes."

"Curt is having an affair."

"Curt may be a lot of things, but he's not a liar!" Heather stated emphatically.

The counselor had heard this kind of defense offered by a hurting spouse many times before. He continued, "I have never been wrong when I have made this accusation. I wouldn't make it lightly. First, let me say there are some things that are always true. The first truth is, *people who commit adultery always lie about it.* Sometimes they think they are being noble, trying not to hurt an innocent party like you. Sometimes they don't want to look like bad guys to their friends. Sometimes they are trying to protect their lovers. In twenty-five years of ministry counseling I have never seen anyone come right out and announce that they were having an affair. Strange, isn't it?"

"I can see why you would think this, but you don't know Curt. He just wouldn't lie to me!" she protested.

"I hope for your sake I am wrong, Heather. I really do. But

let me play back what you have just told me. You told me he has been telling you that he is not sure that he has ever loved you. The reason he can say that now and not during the first five years of your marriage is that he is comparing his current feelings for his mistress with his feelings for you. Up to now he has had nothing to compare your relationship to. In an affair there is literal chemistry. Our bodies release endorphins, a substance that relaxes and calms us down when we make love. The endorphins that a male releases in an affair are incredible. They far exceed the endorphins released when he makes love with his mate. Of course, as time goes by, things even out and the affair isn't such a big deal. It's the law of diminishing returns. But at first it is thrilling, and that makes it hard for a wife to compete. Curt is comparing you to someone else. Of course he loved you when you were married and he continued to love you until recently. Now, he's in la-la-land, under the delusion that he's found true love. Heather, he's changed life patterns: Time away from you and your daughter. That's a sign. He is dressing up for someone, but not for you. He's not coming to you for love.

"As for his car," the counselor continued, "think about it. He could be leaving his car in his parking lot and taking hers. It would be one thing if Curt was just exhibiting one sign of being in an affair, but he exhibits them all. Think about it, and you'll remember something weird that just doesn't add up."

Heather thought for a moment, "There was one thing."

"What?" the counselor pursued with sympathetic interest.

"Well, two weeks ago, Curt went to a Catholic retreat center. He had told me about a month ago that he needed to get away to decide what to do about our marriage. He said he'd found out about this retreat center where you could think things through. He told me he'd made reservations for a weekend. I told him that was fine, because I wanted to get on with our marriage. It was torture being strung along—you know: up in the air. I asked him to leave me the telephone number of the retreat center in case of an emergency. He said it was so private they didn't have a phone and I would just have to wait until he got home. Well, anyway, he went on the retreat."

"But obviously he didn't resolve his question?"

"He came home more confused than ever. But here is the weird part: When he came home, he emptied his suitcase and leaned it up against the bed, but he didn't zip the lid shut. When I went to put it away the lid fell down and a prophylactic fell out. I picked it up and took it into the living room where he was watching TV. I said, 'Curt, what's this?' He said it was a condom. I said, 'That's not what I mean. What's it doing in your suitcase?'"

"He said, 'Remember when we used to use them and I kept them under my side of the bed? And Fluffy [their cat] would get them and bat them around like cat toys? I think one of them was still under the bed and he found it, and was playing with it and took it with him when he slept in the suitcase. Didn't I tell you I found Fluffy sleeping in my suitcase a little while ago?'"

"What did you say to that?" the counselor asked Heather.

"I believed him. It was possible."

The counselor sat silently, waiting for Heather to think a minute about her story and how it had sounded. She did, and suddenly jumped to her feet. Her eyes were as big as saucers when she blurted out, "My husband is having an affair! You must think I'm the biggest idiot in the world!"

"No, Heather, actually I don't. I would describe you as delightfully naive. You are a loving wife. The Bible says, 'Love believes all things.' You love Curt and you have simply wanted to think the best of him. That's all. But now it's time to face the sad truth."

"Should I hire a private detective?"

"You would only spend a lot of money confirming what you already know. Go home tonight, look him in the eye and say, 'Curt, no more games. Don't ask me how I know. I won't tell you. But I know you are having an affair.' Then say, 'I know that when you're ready, you'll tell me. But let's at least both be telling the truth.' Then go into the kitchen and do something and let him think about what you have said. No matter what he says, you say, 'I already know the truth and I'm just waiting to hear it from you.'"

That's just what Heather did. Within two weeks, Curt had confessed to everything. We wish we could tell you this story resolved nicely. It did not. Curt filed for divorce and moved in with his mistress. They were married, then divorced two years later. Heather remarried. With much hard work she is blending her family with her new husband's family. Remarriages are rarely easy arrangements, but she and her new husband are taking the process very seriously.

The preceding story is very representative of what adultery does to families about 85 percent of the time. Heather would have worked on the marriage for the sake of her children, but Curt wouldn't have it because he was still under the delusion that he'd found paradise. Just as often, the offended party feels too betrayed and is too wounded to risk more hurt.

DOUBLE BETRAYAL

Kim and John had been married for ten years. If you had asked John about their marriage, he would have told you, "It has its problems, but it's probably better than most." He wasn't worried about his own position in the marriage, but he was aware that Kim was somehow dissatisfied. He really didn't know how to satisfy her. He just hoped that she would get used to things the way they were. His whole family background declared that people stayed married—happy or not. Divorce was out of the question. He didn't want one and would never have guessed that Kim would want a divorce either.

Kim was far more in touch with her feelings. She knew that she was in trouble. She couldn't survive many more gray mornings, and found herself fantasizing that Prince Charming was coming to rescue her from her mundane existence. She had found herself attracted to other men, but never let them know; nor did she let John know the jeopardy their marriage faced. The more time passed, the easier it became to visualize and accept the dissolution of their marriage.

Then the worst possible thing happened. John and Kim became best friends with Brad and Julie. Brad was an enormously successful businessman, and Julie was his dutiful and dependent wife. Kim became very attracted to Brad and fantasized a Cinderella-like existence with him. If only they had a way of coming together....

Kim experienced a fair amount of guilt for her feelings and shared them with John. She even suggested that they move to the East Coast or change churches so that the temptation might be removed. John heard what she was saying, but he failed to comprehend just how caught up in her fantasy Julie had become. He told her that they would just have to face the problem head-on. They could never run away from Brad. Deep down, John never believed that Brad could betray him. Although he was hurt that his wife was attracted to his best friend, he thought that with time she would get over it.

Brad was as unhappy in his situation as Kim was in hers. He had been seeking relief from his boredom by having out-of-town affairs. Although they were exciting, they didn't fill the void. Like Kim, he had stayed with his marriage because of his children. He had a dwindling Christian faith and had more or less justified his affairs as the better alternative to divorce. The effect, however, was that he was becoming more predisposed to divorce than ever. The bonds were unraveling.

During some unfortunate, unguarded moment, Brad revealed to Kim that he was desperately unhappily married and was grieved that life had dealt him such a boring hand. This was just what Kim had hoped for. She now had the opportunity to live out her fantasy. She quickly revealed that she had had the same feelings about her life; and she risked rejection by confessing to Brad her fantasies about him. Brad confessed that he had deep feelings for Kim, and the affair was launched.

In retrospect, Kim freely admitted that the relationship was based on lust rather than love, but the thrill was back into her existence and there seemed to be no turning back. The exhilaration convinced her that any sacrifice was worth pursuing the relationship.

When the relationship became public, there was an endless stream of pastors and friends who took the time to express their feelings. They told Kim that she was making a horrible mistake. Letters, phone calls, and visits were endured, but her course was set. She patiently tolerated all the well-meaning intentions of her friends. She attempted to justify herself by saying simply, "I need to do this in order to be happy." She freely admitted that she was wrong, but asserted, "God will forgive me for this in time, and whatever he might do to me, it will be worth it!"

Kim and Brad both initiated divorce proceedings against their brokenhearted mates, both of whom would have gladly forgiven them of all their indiscretions.

THE AFTERMATH

From John's perspective, he was experiencing a royal injustice—he called it the "shaft." Kim was driving a Mercedes, eating out at the finest restaurants, holding membership in a country club and a wine tasting club, and traveling extensively all over the world. He was stuck in a lackluster setting, more alone than he had ever been in his life. From John's perspective, Kim had it made. She had everything anyone could ever want, and her life was all hearts and flowers.

Yet, looks are often deceiving. Despite the outward trappings, Kim was experiencing a misery she had never imagined. For more than a year after the divorce, she had the feeling that God had left her for good. She never felt his presence and carried with her a gnawing guilt that ate at her soul like a cancer. She knew no peace, and had a constant sense of condemnation. She had been told that she had committed an unforgivable sin: Because she had married her lover, they would be living in adultery for the rest of their lives.

She told her pastor, "Do you know how I felt? It was like when you walk out on a bright sunshiny day, but you can't see the sun. It was like I was enveloped in my own private night. The worst part of it was that I took it wherever I went. It was just like I had always pictured hell to be.

"I tried to read Scripture, but a terrible feeling came over me whenever I did. I attended all sorts of Christian gatherings, always looking for a way back, but what I heard always made me feel worse.

"I could see what the divorce was doing to my two boys. They were miserable. The youngest cried a lot because he missed his father, and I could also see grief in my oldest. It was tearing them apart, and because I was remarried there was no way to undo the harm I had done. It was obvious that the boys resented their stepfather and would never accept him. I didn't feel close to Brad's children. There was always tension in our home. I have come to accept that things will always be like this. We will never know a close-knit family again. It's just the way it is with stepfamilies.

"Since Brad and I came into the marriage as adulterers, we have always wondered whether the other would remain faithful. It is a haunting feeling that comes and goes, but it never goes for very long. I am especially uneasy when he goes on business trips, and he is uneasy when we are socializing with good-looking married men. Insecurity is not a good foundation for a remarriage.

"We lost nearly all our close friends, so we had to start all over again. I hated to see people who had known me as John's wife, and avoided them at all costs. This was a great sadness, because we really had some special friends. It was lonely for a long time. I still feel shame when I see friends who know what I did. It just isn't something about which you can ever be proud."

Kim's pastor asked if she thought it was worth it, and Kim quickly answered, "It's never worth it to cross God."

Then he asked her if she thought she had found what she was looking for when she left John. She paused for a long time and said with a definite air of sadness in her voice, "I don't know."

Brad and Kim will never be proud or feel good about what they did. But they have tried to take the steps left open to them to salvage as much of their integrity as possible. Brad wrote a letter to John ten years after the divorce, and John responded. Notice the regret and pain reflected in these letters and ask yourself, "Wouldn't it have been better if they had never gotten into this situation in the first place?"

Dear John,

Many years have passed by. Nonetheless, I feel I must deal in whatever way I can with the wrong I have done to you and the hurt and pain I brought into your life.

It's difficult for me now to comprehend how I could have hurt so many people, including a wife who loved me, my children, and my best friend—passion can really be blinding. Kim and I have carried a lot of guilt. We feel the Lord, in his compassion, has forgiven us; but there will always be scars as reminders. We are especially thankful that the kids have come through as well as they have, but we realize there are many tough years ahead. They will need our prayers and tender guidance.

Anyway, old friend, I wanted to write this letter to sincerely apologize to you for the horrible wrong I committed. There are no excuses—you were always a good and caring friend. I just let myself get caught up and would not put on the brakes. Frankly, I don't know if I could bring myself to offer forgiveness if the situation were reversed, but I am led to ask forgiveness from you.

Sincerely,
Brad

Dear Brad,

It's been about four months since I received your letter and I need to respond. I did not answer sooner because, frankly, I really never expected an apology from you and had no clue as to how to reply.

First things first. You are and have been forgiven by me for about two years.

It took that long for the Lord to bring me to the place where I could see that my hatred for you and what you did was destroying my life. At that point, because God commanded it, and because it was consuming me, I gave in and forgave. Since then my life has improved.

Your letter has caused me to reflect on the past ten years. The two things that stand out the most are the loss of my boys and being betrayed.

The times you now take for granted with Dale and Eric are moments that should have been mine. The good, the bad, the happy and the sad times are all times that should have been mine. I'll never retrieve that time and neither will my sons.

Betrayal is hard to recover from. The two people I trusted and loved the most hurt me. For some reason, Brad, I have always felt that you were always more responsible than Kim for the circumstances. She had tried to warn me, and I never heard it—but our friendship was somehow special, and I put far too much faith in it and never saw what was going on. You really blindsided me. Until recently, I have had a very hard time getting close to another male.

This letter has turned out to be much more personal than I thought it would be. There was a long period when I was sure that I would never recover, but let me tell you what God has done. I have been blessed far beyond what I ever could have hoped for; my relationship with Ellen is quite special—it's what I always pictured marriage being. Kurt [John and Ellen's son] is super. Through him, God is giving me back the years I missed with Dale and Eric. And the relationship I do have with Dale and Eric is warm and loving and extremely close.

Brad, thank you for your letter. I know it was hard for you to write and I appreciate it.

Asking my forgiveness is probably the easiest part of the process. Seeing the results of your actions has got to be the tough part. There was a long time my fondest desire was to see you burn in hell for what you did. It's taken the Lord a long time to bring us both around—but he has and I no longer feel ill will toward you. In fact, I often miss our friendship. I pray the Lord will bless you and give you peace of mind.

John

Clearly the predator of adultery is far better contained before it attacks than after.

WORKING THROUGH ADULTERY

Making the decision to work on a marriage after an affair will require careful thought. Remember that one short-term affair does not constitute a pattern and does not necessarily indicate that the offending party will ever offend again. But two affairs are considered a pattern, and the victim of the affair must know that their mate is likely to have affairs over and over again throughout the life of the marriage. Affairs are addicting, beckoning the addict to repeat the folly.

We have seen some remarkable healing in our work with couples who have committed themselves to reconciliation. When commitment is high, there is hope. When humility and forgiveness are part of the plan, there is hope. When there is a deep desire to grow, in spite of the pain, the broken trust, and the fear that follows adultery, there is hope.

If you have decided to reconcile with your mate, here are some steps that have helped others navigate these turbulent waters:

Assignment for the adulterer:

1. *Remove the third party from your life.* No contact whatsoever can be tolerated.

2. *Your mate must be sure that the inappropriate relationship is over.* We suggest that you call the person with whom you were in a relationship and, while your mate is listening, tell them that the relationship is over and to please not attempt contact of any kind. You must make clear that you are serious about working on your marriage.

3. *You must repent to God and to your mate.* Don't have an attitude of entitlement, saying things like, "You have to forgive me," or, "You owe me." Return to the marriage with a *no-excuses* attitude, and be prepared for your mate to be angry, hurt, and distrusting for some time. Do not underestimate the damage and fear that come after adultery. You may have to say you're sorry for months before you are believed. Remember, trust was destroyed and needs to be rebuilt. That may take some time. Don't put limits on the time it takes.

4. *We suggest you become close and accountable to a mature Christian.* Weekly prayer with an accountability group; instruction in *doing right*; and, in some cases, professional counseling and involvement in a support group for sexual addiction are possibilities to be explored.

5. *Since the vows are broken, it is necessary to court your mate.* You must bring a sense of freshness and starting over to the relationship. That will mean a rekindling process. Dating, thoughtful cards, flowers, affection, gentleness, patience, or anything else that encourages romance will help your mate to see your true heart and sincerity. We recommend you never cease this new courting process, even as the healing occurs.

Assignment for the victim of adultery:

1. *If you choose to stay with your mate* to work out the problems of the marriage, *you must forgive him or her* to the best of your ability. That may be a process, rather than an event. You may have to tell him or her over and over *and over* that you are still hurting, but trying to let the past go.

2. *Remember that an affair is very addicting,* and letting go of it is a process, not an event. It usually happens in two stages. First, contact is broken; then the feelings slowly die.

3. *Compliment and appreciate your mate whenever he or she does something that truly makes you happy.* If, in your pain, you continue to play the part of the victim as your mate attempts to change and reconcile, you're not doing your part. If you realize that you have brought your mate back only to punish him or her, call off the process. It is doomed to fail. If you are sincerely wanting the reconciliation, seek out someone who supports your goal for your marriage to succeed. Spend time often with this friend or couple, so that they can encourage you to hope for the best. Give them reasons to love you. Look nice, be positive and supportive of their efforts.

4. *Be willing to push for professional help if it is needed.* At first this may be for yourself, in order to be strengthened. At the beginning or later, it may be necessary for both you and your mate. Be sure to make clear requests about using this resource.

SHOULD I OR SHOULDN'T I?

You may find yourself wondering what to do if your mate commits adultery. Will it be divorce or reconciliation? If you seek counsel, it will be the luck of the draw, so to speak. Some pastors or counselors will ask you to stay in the marriage and work it out. Others will tell you to dump the bum or junk the witch. Even when you go to the Bible or to God in prayer, you will quickly discover that there is no clear direction. God gives you permission to go or stay. You will not be punished for going, nor applauded for staying. In this one peculiar circumstance he leaves it up to you to decide, and you must make the decision with all of its difficult implications.

One thing is sure. God does not put you in a position to be double-victimized, even if some well-meaning pastors, counselors, and friends might unwittingly do so. If you came to us, we would encourage you to try again if your mate had a short-term affair, took full responsibility for the adultery, broke off the relationship to the third party, and repented of the sin with contrition and humility. That advice would depend on your first telling us you wanted to reconcile.

As we have discussed this subject in the past, we have disclosed to each other the decisions that each of us have made with our mates. We found that we as couples—Gary and Carol, and Tom and Lisa—independently made decisions about this topic prior to our marriages. Each of us as couples made the same decision. None of the four of us would be allowed the foolish luxury of an affair. We have all understood that from the beginning. In our cases, to break the promises we made before God and witnesses would mean the end of the marriage. Perhaps we made these decisions because of our roles as teachers, knowing that much was expected of us. Also, the decision serves as a constant reminder that we are not exempt from temptation nor the sin of adultery. All are vulnerable. Gary and Carol have been married for thirty-one years. Tom and Lisa have been married for eleven. We believe our decisions about how to handle an affair have helped keep us faithful—with the help of God. This decision has served as a *preven-tion* and a *warning* for our weaker moments.

We deeply value our marriages. While forgiveness for adultery is always a possibility, the final decision remains with the mate. We are not in support of divorce, but of marriage. However, if you or your mate ever make the serious mistake of committing adultery, you will have single-handedly brought the question of divorce to bear. We hope neither you nor we will ever have to face this decision. End of subject.

SIXTEEN

∾

Breaking the Cycle:
Verbal, Physical, and Sexual Abuse

Many of you who read this chapter are the victims of verbal, physical, or sexual abuse in your marriage. Some of you reading this chapter are the abusers. Some of you may find yourselves in a mutually abusive or coaddictive relationship. We will address what you can do to end this destructive cycle, regardless of which position you hold in the abusive relationship.

If you are a victim of abuse, whether it be verbal, physical, or sexual, we know that even reading this chapter will provoke anxiety in you if you are currently in the abuse cycle. Please find an emotionally safe place where you can read without interruption or fear of more abuse.

VERBAL ABUSE

Verbal abuse. We've all heard it. It's those words that make us cringe, the low blow. It's the negative insult that plays over and over like a broken record. It is the spirit-crushing remark that keeps you from trying. It is the discouraging word that keeps you from wanting to get up in the morning. It's the humiliating comment that makes you feel unworthy to face your friends. It's the crippling statement that makes you wonder if you might be in danger. It's the weapon used to hurt and control.

Verbal abuse eats away at the foundation and supports of love in your marriage in the same way that termites eat away at the foundation and supports of your home. Without sufficient supports your relationship will come crashing down.

What does verbal abuse sound like? Verbal abuse resonates several sounds. None of them are pleasant. They vary in dissonance, volume, and intensity. Some of those sounds are more frightening and debilitating that others. We have all marveled at how a high-pitched sound can shatter a valuable piece of crystal. Such is the power of verbal abuse.

Here are ten types of verbal abuse:

1. *Demeaning words:* Insults and digs that sting and crush.
2. *Profane words:* Name calling and exclamations that insult in the lowest form.
3. *Filibustering:* Long, condescending lectures—where the recipient can't get a word in edgewise.
4. *Untimely criticism:* For the sake of humiliating and embarrassing.
5. *Threats:* Words that inspire fear and haunt the future.
6. *Injuring with the truth:* Speaking truth, but leaving the love out.
7. *Yelling, and harsh tones and noises:* The voice of intimidation.
8. *The silent treatment:* Silence used to control and demean.
9. *Sarcasm:* Biting statements that reveal hidden anger.
10. *Lying with half-truths:* Confusing and distorting reality, often by exaggerating or minimizing.

When a person is subjected to this kind of verbal treatment on a regular basis, he or she will experience harm. Verbal abuse is more subtle than physical or sexual abuse, and for that reason gets less negative press. But don't be fooled, it can be just as destructive to your sense of self and to your marriage relationship. Over the years the two of us have had to help repair the damage done by this type of abuse. It should not be tolerated.

In order to clarify what verbal abuse looks like, let's listen in on actual recordings of two couples, which reveal that both men and women can verbally abuse their spouses.

The heartcracker suite. Laura was thirty-four, but she felt fifty. She and Larry had been married for seven years, but she had never felt cherished or nourished. She longed for an intimate connection with her husband.

Laura heard the engine of their Ford Mustang rumble into the driveway and the door slam shut. Automatically, she felt her body tense, knowing that seconds from now she would be hearing the usual refrain.

The door opened. "Laura, what kinda neighbors do you want us to be, anyway? There's a big brown spot in the front lawn! Why did you let it get that way? I should never have trusted you to talk to the gardeners about the lawn! I *knew* you'd screw it up!"

Laura found herself feeling disoriented. She had not seen the lawn. Following a well-worn pattern for surviving Larry's onslaughts, she responded, "I'm sorry, Larry. I guess I should have noticed it."

He interrupted her apology and shouted, "Come on, Laura. I work my butt off all week providing for this family, and you can't even take care of the menial tasks on our 150-by-200-foot property? Homemaker? You? Give me a break! You wanted to stay home and take care of the family? Well, when are you gonna do it? I'll tell you something else. If I handled my career the way you run this home, I'd be fired. Maybe I should fire you!"

Laura began to tremble. She couldn't get her words out. Only a stutter was emitted from her mouth.

Immediately, Larry mimicked her stutter, and escalated his barrage of words. "You're such a wimp. Stammering won't work with me. Stop manipulating me and acting scared again."

Laura *was* scared! She sought the refuge of her upstairs bedroom, but before she could reach the stairway in hopes of making an escape, Larry blocked her way.

"Don't you walk away from me. I'm not done talking to you! Sit down! I have a few things to say to you. The lawn's not the only thing that looks bad around here! You've put on at least ten pounds, or is it twenty? I didn't marry a fatso and I won't live with one! You're not only fat, but you're lazy. Things are slipping. What do I have to do to get your attention! What's it gonna take?"

Laura had laid her face in her hands, now wet with tears. She started to ask what he wanted from her. Again Larry cut her off. "If I'm gonna tell you what I want, you better get a notepad. You can't remember anything I ever tell you for more than a second."

Laura composed herself. Walking toward the kitchen, she met Larry's harsh response, "Where do you think you're going?"

Laura turned to face the wall and said, "To get a notepad and a pencil. Maybe I do forget, and need to write things down. I'm really, really sorry."

Revelling in the power he had over Laura, Larry maintained a sinister smile. After sitting for two hours under his relentless accusations and insults, Laura felt numb and exhausted. She barely heard most of his comments. Instead, the fear overtook her ability to listen to the words and all she heard was percussion, volume, and intensity.

A thousand times she fantasized leaving the relationship, but Larry threatened that if she ever tried, he would take the children and hurt her in ways that she could never imagine. Laura felt trapped and resorted to waiting once again for the storm to pass.

It was Larry's hunger that caused him to finally break a long, heavy silence and demand, "What does somebody have to do to get dinner around here? I'll go take a shower, and I'm hoping for something decent to eat when I come down the stairs. I'll eat in the family room. There's a Lakers game on tonight!"

Below the belt. John and Elaine had thought twice about inviting Brett and Brenda to the New Year's Eve party. Unlike most of their friends, Brett and Brenda posed a constant threat of creating a scene. They were fairly confident that Brett would not provoke an incident, but they couldn't remember a time when Brenda *hadn't* created a major disturbance, interrupting the entire party.

Brett was always the unwitting victim of a wrath that no one could understand. Why was Brenda always so demeaning? She found words to humiliate Brett in every area of his life. John asked Elaine, "Wasn't it last Halloween that Brenda nearly wrecked the evening?"

Elaine chuckled, saying, "Yeah, I remember when they first arrived at the door. Brett was dressed as a tramp. The first words out of Brenda's mouth were, 'Elaine, I'm sorry we couldn't find a costume for Brett!'"

John said, "I remember that later in the evening, when Eric told us he had just gotten a pit bull for his wife, Brenda shouted out, 'I wish I could make a trade like that for Brett!'"

John and Elaine realized that under the humor was a mean-spirited tone of sarcasm. John recalled that while others laughed, Brett winced, looking visibly hurt. He rarely laughed anymore. The worst incident they remembered was Brenda's inappropriate disclosure about Brett's recent probation for poor job performance. They had noticed that he seemed depressed, and weren't too surprised that it was affecting his job.

She boldly proclaimed the news to the group at their party, "Did you all hear about Brett's job? They put him on probation 'cause he just isn't cutting it! I've been thinking about putting him on probation at home." With venomous sarcasm she added, "His job isn't the only place he's not cuttin' it!"

John said, "If you think Brenda is caustic at parties, you

should see her in action in their own home! When I was there last month helping Brett install the dishwasher, she hovered over the project and never let up on Brett the whole time. I asked him, 'Why do you put up with this? Is she always like this?'"

Sheepishly, Brett responded, "I don't really know. I just know I haven't been happy for a long time."

Guests began to arrive at the New Year's party, bringing a delectable variety of dishes for the potluck supper. The house began to fill with laughter and rich conversation. The doorbell rang again, and when Elaine opened the door, there stood Brenda—alone. Elaine gazed past her and inquired, "Is Brett parking the car?"

Brenda smiled as if nothing was wrong. With aloofness she proclaimed, "Brett has moved back home with his parents. Who needs him?"

Elaine stepped outside, closing the door behind her. She began, "You may come to the party tonight, but neither John nor I want you to use this as an opportunity to put down Brett like you've done in the past. Brenda, we like Brett. We will not listen to verbal abuse about him."

Brenda's quick temper flared. She glared into Elaine's eyes. "I don't need Brett and I don't need you guys either!" She promptly stormed off and sped away in her car.

John stepped outside and Elaine told him what had happened. While he felt pity for Brenda and Brett, he commended Elaine, saying, "I support you 100 percent. *True friends don't put up with put-downs!* I know that was hard for you. I know you had to speak the truth. I think I'll go call Brett and get him to come over. No doubt he needs his friends right now."

What can you do? If these stories sound all too familiar, you are a victim of verbal abuse. It is time for changes that will make a difference. It's time to assess your marital relationship to ascertain what steps are necessary for promoting healthy interaction and no longer tolerating abuse. The cycle can be broken through skill-building or through intensive counseling. A qualified counselor can assist you in designing the steps needed to save or strengthen and perpetuate your marriage. If you like, you can skip ahead to the section, "Breaking the Cycle," beginning on page 247.

PHYSICAL ABUSE

Following is a list of actions performed on and against the will of the mate. All are abusive. None of them belong within a marriage nor any other relationship. We are saddened to tell you that all of these behaviors *and more* have actually occurred in the lives of the men and women we have counseled:

- Raising the arm or fist in a threatening gesture
- Pointing the index finger, waved forcefully in the face
- Jabbing the index finger forcefully against the chest
- Restricting or impeding freedom of movement
- Pushing or shoving
- Striking of the body (slapping, hitting, kicking, scratching, or pinching to injure)
- Physical restraining of the mate
- Striking with objects of any kind
- Cutting or burning, or threats to cut or burn
- Throwing objects to frighten or injure the partner
- Choking, threatening to choke, or using a choke hold
- Waving of knives to threaten (stabbing, slashing, or threatening to stab or slash)
- Threats to the body (a threat to disfigure, endanger, injure, or kill)
- Demanding and forcing the partner to ingest drugs
- Hair pulling
- Dragging

- Pointing or firing a gun to threaten
- Smothering or holding under water
- Stalking
- Locking into confined spaces; locking out of the house

A note to you, the reader: Out of consideration to those of you who have experienced any of the above or some other unmentioned acts of physical abuse, we will avoid offering an account of the more graphic and hideous acts of violence that too many unfortunate marital partners have presented to us as counselors. We realize that reading an account can trigger memories in the minds of survivors of these actions. In no way do we wish to re-traumatize you.

We will cite an account of physical abuse. You may decide to discontinue reading this chapter due to your own sensitivity to the subject matter. If you know that you are emotionally vulnerable at this time, we invite you to turn now to page 247 to read the section "Breaking the Cycle." There we will instruct you and reinforce you to free yourself from the threat and violence of physical abuse.

Descent into darkness. Teri sat in her Toyota van, hesitant to start the engine. If she started the engine, she would have to put it in gear. If she put it in gear, she would head toward home. She didn't want to go home. Home hadn't been a safe place for years. But going home was inevitable. Sighing deeply, she started the engine.

It was Saturday afternoon. She was hoping that Mitchell would still be engrossed with college football. The Ohio Buckeyes were playing Michigan State, and he had told Teri only an hour ago, "Why don't you go shopping and get out of my hair. Let me watch my game in peace!"

It wouldn't have occurred to Teri to cross Mitchell. She nodded and headed toward the market. Although being at the market provided a safe distance from Mitchell, it carried with it its own kind of anxiety. What if she picked the wrong cereal and set him off? What if the melon was overly ripe? What if the steak turned out to be tough? What if she spent more money on groceries than he wanted? She had been hit by Mitchell for offenses smaller than these.

Teri had managed to be free from abuse for four days now. She was doing her best to calculate what had made the difference. Had she been kinder? Or quieter? Or more efficient? She wasn't sure. She wished with all of her heart that she could navigate through the minefield of Mitchell's emotions. She thought in terms of his favorites whenever she made a decision. She would do anything to please him, if only she knew how. Sometimes Teri condemned herself, thinking, "Six years should be enough time to learn how to please your husband. What's wrong with me? I can't seem to do that!"

The cart was nicely filled with items chosen to please Mitchell. As she watched the checker scan the groceries, her heart began to pound and she second-guessed her food selections. Her muscles tensed as she wrote the check. The total amount was greater than anticipated. Teri was tempted to return some of the items, but she couldn't bring herself to chance the disapproval of the checker.

She unloaded her cart of groceries into the van and noticed the receipt in clear view on top of one of the bags. She wadded it up and threw it underneath the car. "No use giving Mitchell hard evidence!"

On the way home, Teri drove under the speed limit. She wasn't in a hurry. In fact, when she saw her own residence, she drove right on by. She talked herself into going to the Baskin Robbins 31 Flavors ice cream parlor to indulge in a chocolate, macadamia nut double-scoop ice cream cone. Mitchell liked strawberry, and she had them hand-pack a pint for him as a peace offering. She placed it on the chair next to her while she devoured her favorite flavor. Unfortunately, when she left the ice cream parlor, she also left behind Mitchell's strawberry ice cream.

As she approached her home this time, she entered the driveway, reached toward the visor and pressed the button on the garage door opener. She opened the door leading into the kitchen, and began carrying the groceries to the kitchen counter. It was her personal ritual. Mitchell had never helped, not once. Mitchell was sprawled on the couch. She could sense his angry eyes drilling a hole in the back of her head. As she turned to look, Mitchell rose menacingly and hissed, "Where the hell have you been?"

She'd had the misfortune of coming home during half-time. She thought, "Oh, if only I hadn't gone for the ice cream. I timed this wrong!" Mitchell hated to listen to college bands and watch what he considered air-headed cheerleaders. So, she now had his formidable and undivided attention. Teri stammered, "I went shopping. That's what you wanted me to do, wasn't it?"

"I didn't expect you to be gone all day! What took you so long? Did you clean out the mall, too?" he accused, waving his finger at her.

In an effort to put her peace offering on the table quickly, Teri said, "I stopped by Baskin Robbins and got you some strawberry ice cream."

He smirked sarcastically and began searching through the bags of groceries. "Where is it, anyway? I can't find it!"

She gasped as she recalled leaving it at the ice cream parlor. But instead of telling him the truth, she began to tear open the bags, attempting to appear upset at the server for not giving her the carton. "I can't believe they didn't give me that ice cream!"

Interrupting her, Mitchell screamed, "There's no ice cream because you went somewhere else. Where did you really go, liar?!"

"That's where I went—to 31 Flavors, just like I said. It's gotta be here somewhere."

No sooner had she finished her sentence than he shoved her

and hurled her directly against the open pantry door. A shock wave went through her body as her forehead hit first. She heard the telling snap of her rib as it crashed against the doorknob. Then she slumped down to the floor.

Mitchell rushed in and kicked her twice. "Maybe now you're ready to tell me the truth. Where have you been and who were you with?"

Teri propped herself up against the kitchen drawers and pleaded for mercy with her eyes. She knew that no words would assuage his violent temper. He kicked her again. The biting pain ripped through her system. Looking up, she said, "Mitch, I went shopping alone. I promise!"

Now, totally enraged, Mitch slapped her face and grabbed her by the hair, dragging her across the floor at an incredible speed. He heaved open the sliding glass door and then threw her savagely onto the brick patio, yelling, "Get the hell outta my sight, B——!"

Teri attempted unsuccessfully to get up. She dragged herself over to the redwood patio chair, and used it to climb to a standing position. Limping her way along the walkway, she braced herself against the side of the garage. Teri was relieved to see the garage door still open. The keys and her purse were still inside the van. She struggled into the driver's seat and backed out of the garage. Desperately, she headed to the community hospital, afraid all the while that her broken rib might puncture her lung. Every breath produced a wrenching pain in her side. She pulled down the rear-view mirror and noticed that the left side of her face was covered with blood.

In the emergency room at the hospital, Teri was questioned about the nature of her injuries. She answered, "This is so embarrassing. You won't believe it—I'm so clumsy. I was carrying groceries up a flight of stairs to my apartment and I slipped on the top step. I'm probably lucky to be alive." A battle-wearied head nurse locked eyes with Teri and said, "You're right, honey. I don't believe it. Get out before he does kill you!" She was treated and released.

The sad truth about physical abuse. We wish we could honestly tell you that this is an unusual story; however, it is all too common. In Gary's ministry to single parents, one out of every two women report having been hit by their mate with a closed fist on at least one occasion. The sad and shocking truth is that physical abuse is rarely a one-time incident. Physical abuse escalates over long periods of time.

Once out of an abusive relationship, many victims ask, "Why did I wait so long to get out?" Only the victim of abuse can answer that question. Victims have their own distorted rationale which keep them in this dark situation.

If you are in a physically abusive relationship, we agree as a therapist and pastor that it is essential that you remove yourself (and your children) from the imminent dangers of abuse. *Now is the time.* Later will be too late!

Beware of uninformed advice from friends, relatives, pastors, and counselors who are unfamiliar with the realities of physical abuse. Again, we plead with pastors *especially* to work from an informed position with this unique and potentially deadly situation. The abused women you advise are somebody's precious daughters and the abused men (yes, men!) are somebody's cherished sons. Of course they are also highly esteemed of God.

We would like to remind you that adultery is named in Scripture as a sin against the flesh. Is there any question that physical abuse is scorned by God as a sin against the flesh? Pastors, friends, relatives, and counselors, *don't you dare send an abused person back into this kind of nightmare!* The more we all know about the violence of physical abuse, the more responsible we all must become as dedicated and courageous leaders in the protection of those under our direction and care.

We strongly encourage you to now turn to page 247 and read the section "Breaking the Cycle." Here you will find encouragement and instruction for ending the torment of physical abuse. Knowing what to do and following those steps may save your life!

SEXUAL ABUSE IN MARRIAGE

Some words just don't belong together. *Sexual abuse* and *marriage* are those kinds of words. They seem to address diametrically opposed ideas—one is loving and cherishing, the other is hurtful and destructive. Unfortunately, for too many women, these words *do* fit together and they accurately describe the tragic encounters they have endured.

A marriage vow is made, beginning a sacred unity between two people. That unity encompasses the physical, spiritual, emotional, and intellectual aspects of each partner. Sexual abuse is an assault against the whole person, physically, intellectually, emotionally, and spiritually.

Sexual abuse occurs when one partner is forced to have sex with the other partner. It has no place in anyone's life—especially within the sanctity of marriage. Sexual abuse is a humiliating, assaultive, and violent crime! If sexual abuse occurred outside of the marriage, it would be considered assault and battery. Why is it tolerated within the sacred confines of marriage?

How does sexual abuse happen? How does a relationship that initially seemed loving and tender decline into the darkness of sexual abuse? Why was abusive behavior allowed to continue and eventually escalate? When tenderness is only an external action and is not founded on love, it serves merely as a manipulation. The true test of love comes when stress occurs or as disagreements surface. With authentic love, stress, and conflict call into action attitudes in search of agreeable solutions. Where tenderness was just a facade, stress reveals its thin veil. Behind it are found arrogance, disregard, and hatefulness. We are not referring to a fleeting disrespect or disregard for a specific action, which can be part of healthy conflict. This is an accumulating resentment and disrespect for the *person*. This intensifying disregard finds expression through mean-spirited actions, as seen in this diagram:

Disrespect —>Control and Manipulation——>Tolerated Abuse

The seeds of abuse are planted in the soil of disrespect. People who sexually abuse their partners do not love their mates; they are motivated by fear: fear of losing control and fear of inadequacy. These deep-seated feelings of fear and inadequacy fuel the perceived need to control. The need for control rules supreme. That desperate need drives the person to take charge and promote himself at *any* cost—even the cost of his partner's wholeness.

Sexual abuse in marriage always includes a verbal attack, characterized by demeaning words and threats. These include put-downs about the spouse's body. Not only is the innocent partner vulnerable physically, but emotionally as well. The abusive words are aimed at the partner within the privacy of the bedroom, piercing the heart. The seeds of disrespect have grown into hostile words and actions.

The source of the abusive partner's control and manipulation is the abused partner's internal sense of shame and fear. Repeated acts of force, demands of every conceivable kind, and threats for noncompliance destroy the abused partner's sense of safety and of self. The abused partner is treated like an object, not a person. Hope for change diminishes with each subsequent assault. The verbal abuse often escalates into physical abuse, and includes all of the acts of physical abuse discussed earlier. Additionally, these acts of physical abuse are brought into the sexual relationship, and unleashed on the partner.

How do I know whether I have been sexually abused?

Circle yes or no for each question below. Yes answers are signs that you are in an abusive sexual relationship in your marriage.

Yes No 1. Do you engage in sexual activity with your partner against your will?

Yes No 2. Do you engage in sexual activity with your partner in the midst of verbal abuse such as threats, put-downs, or intimidations?

Yes No 3. Do you engage in sexual activity with your partner in the midst of physical abuse (restraining, hitting, shoving)?

Yes No 4. Do you engage in sexual activity with your partner by demand?

Yes No 5. Does your partner intentionally injure you physically during sexual activity?

Yes No 6. Do you feel like an object and experience emotional pain following sexual activity with your partner?

Any *yes* answers to the above questions are strong indicators that you need to take steps to break the cycle of sexual abuse in your marriage. Please read the next section, "Breaking the Cycle," and take action immediately. Practical help is offered. There is hope. There are solutions. By following the steps given, you will be on your way to freedom from this lonely and frightening lifestyle.

BREAKING THE CYCLE

Why would anyone become trapped in the web of verbal, physical, or sexual abuse within the marriage? There are two strong explanations: terror, and more terror. For some women (and in rare instances, for men) this abuse represents a repeated nightmare. They were caught in the grip of abuse and terror as children, and now find themselves tolerating it in their marriage.

Other times, the intimidation of repeated abuse chisels away at an otherwise strong partner Until he or she gives up the fight. Their response is one of *learned helplessness*. They feel helpless in the face of the abuse and believe they have no hope of controlling the negative events in their life. In the case of verbal, physical, or sexual abuse, the physical and verbal threats for not complying lead to intense feelings of helplessness. Compliance becomes survival. To provoke the abuser further only escalates the abuse. The compliance becomes a combination of agreeing with the abuser, conforming to the force, trying to please, allowing the self to be violated, all in hopes that the abuser's demands will be satisfied so that the abuse will cease.

The predator of abuse will not go away on its own. It seeks to devour. If you live with an abuser, we encourage you to address this problem head-on. We want to introduce you to a method of taking on a predator.

Facing a predator does not come naturally. The worst mistake you can make is to turn your back on him or her. A predator won't go away. Most of the time, you can't outrun one. Learn what Gary learned at the zoo. Learn the *alpha attitude*. The alpha attitude is essentially maintaining a confident stance, a posture that reflects that you are *more than equal* to the predator you are facing. Alpha means *first place, most dominant, strongest member*. In any grouping of animals, the alpha animal will be the least threatened one. You must come to the place where you will no longer tolerate the predatory behavior of your mate's abuse. Remember, we get what we tolerate. Abuse is not to be tolerated.

Chances are that long-term subjection to verbal abuse has weakened your confidence in your own power to stand against the abuse. That simply means you will need to look for help. Thankfully, much is known about breaking the cycle of abuse. Help is available for you.

Awareness of abuse is the beginning of ending the abuse cycle. The first step in breaking the cycle of abuse is to get help, to tell someone about what you are experiencing. It is almost impossible to break the cycle alone. You need and deserve the support of others on a continuous basis until you have recovered your strength and hope once again.

You are about to learn the steps that will be necessary if you are to end the darkness of abuse in your life.

Abuse must be stopped! Abuse offenders believe that their actions are justified. As we review the common characteristics of abusers, we must point out that *reasoning will not solve the problem*. People who fit this description are not reasonable. Abusers exhibit:

1. *Poor impulse control:* They act without thinking.

2. *High dependency:* They cannot meet their intense needs independently.

3. *Drug or alcohol abuse:* Substance distorts their reality and reduces their impulse control.

4. *Rigidity:* They will not reason. They insist that they are right.

5. *Authoritarianism:* They expect their mate to follow their rules unquestioningly.

6. *Value for physical punishment as method of control:* They justify abusive actions as necessary and appropriate.

7. *A tendency to view spouse as property and as an object:* They lack empathy and don't see the spouse as a person with thoughts, opinions, feelings, or value. They only see their partner in light of what he or she can do to meet their selfish needs and demands.

Since offenders do not respond to reason or discussion, the actions for stopping the abuse will not depend on cooperation from the abuser. If there were cooperation, there would be no abuse. To effectively stop the cycle, we recommend that you follow these steps:

1. *Recognize that you cannot do this alone.*

2. *Contact support:* A professional counselor, a minister trained in dealing with abuse, a women's shelter, or an abuse support group, through community, women's, or church organizations.

3. *Make an appointment:* Meet with a qualified helping professional or support group leader immediately.

4. *Tell the truth about your situation:* This will feel very risky. Remember, silence is riskier. Without help, the situation will only get worse. Take this step of faith.

5. *Follow the direction you are given by those who have been there before with others like yourself:* They know the process and can guide you. You will strengthen under their guidance.

WHAT DO I HAVE TO LOOK FORWARD TO?

Obtaining help may save your life. Abuse escalates over time. It becomes more intense and more dangerous. Worse yet, your ability to recover will diminish with each subsequent incident of abuse.

Obtaining help will create realistic hope for your future. There is hope. For that hope to be real, things will have to change. You must do something different. What that *is* depends on your situation, your personality, and your current skills. With qualified help, you will be able to assess the best plan to follow to make the difference—to break the cycle. Much has happened to reduce your life of hope to a life of fear, but there is a pathway back.

Obtaining help will provide support for the journey. You deserve support. It will help you to know you are not alone. It will help you gain the strength and courage you need to be part of breaking the cycle.

> "For I know the plans I have for you," declares the Lord, "plans to prosper you and not to harm you, plans to give you hope and a future."   **Jeremiah 29:11**

Taking that first step. We want to direct you toward help. We hope we have helped you identify your need and have spurred you to action. However, you cannot tackle abuse alone. Your success will depend on specialized skills and support. Do not hesitate. Take the first step by calling a resource that can team up with you in this difficult and courageous process. Contact your local church, YMCA, college or university, women's center, or community center for reputable referrals to counselors, pastors, and support groups.

APPENDIX A

∾

What If My Spouse or I Have an Addiction?

I f you or your mate are involved in an addiction, there is a
recovery journey ahead. It is essential that you waste no
time getting started. There is caring and effective help for both
the addict and his or her mate. Understanding your own
addiction and the steps to freedom is primary. Understanding
your mate's addiction will ensure that you are not inadvertently
contributing to the problem. To break an addiction you will
need help.

Addictions that often show up in counselors' offices include:

Alcohol	Drugs
Gambling	Eating
Prescription drugs	Spending
Relationships	Sex
Raging	

If you or your mate are obsessed by any of the above behaviors and say that it's not a problem, that you can stop any time
you want to, but you or your mate do not stop, then you are
addicted. Help is required for you to turn this behavior around
and become free from it.

Ignoring addiction leads to more serious levels of addiction
and more destructive consequences. The predator of addiction
has a devastating effect on the marriage relationship. The sooner a person gets help, the better.

In addition to any individual help you might obtain, we

253

urge you to seek one of the twelve-step programs listed below. These programs are concrete, focused, consistent, and effective. Local contacts are available through your telephone directory, or you can call the national headquarters. These organizations can give you specific information regarding recovery, and can direct you to a support group in your area. These support groups are offered free of charge.

The twelve-step programs are available nationwide. That may be your first step. Or contact your pastor, a counselor, or a community center. Whatever you do, do something to obtain competent help. There is hope for you, your marriage, and your children in seeking recovery. The first step is the hardest.

Sources of Help: The Twelve-Step Model

Alcoholics Anonymous World Services, Inc.
P.O. Box 459, Grand Central Station
New York, NY 10163
(212) 686-1100

Al-Anon Family Group Headquarters
1372 Broadway
New York, NY 10018
(212) 302-7240

Debtors Anonymous
314 West 53rd Street
New York, NY 10018
(212) 969-0710

Gamblers Anonymous
P.O. Box 17173
Los Angeles, CA 90017
(213) 386-8769

Incest Survivors Anonymous
P.O. Box 17245
Long Beach, CA 90807-7245
(310) 428-5599

Narcotics Anonymous, World Service Office
16155 Wyandotte Street
Van Nuys, CA 91406
(818) 780-3951

National Association for Children of Alcoholics
38706 Coast Highway, Suite 201
South Laguna, CA 92677
(714) 499-3889

Overcomers Outreach
2290 West Whittier Boulevard, Suite A/D
La Habra, CA 90631
(310) 697-3994

Overeaters Anonymous, World Service Office
2190 190th Street
Torrance, CA 90504
(310) 542-8368

APPENDIX B

∾

How Do We Plan a Budget?

Money management begins with a budget. The advantage of planning is knowing in advance what you will need. Then, when income is earned, it can be distributed wisely. It is all too easy to fall into the trap of spending as you go, then running low in the end. For some, that happens at the end of the month; for others, it happens at the end of the day! Here is a recommended budget. (You will need to adjust the percentages according to your own needs and geographical area. The percentages for housing are considerably higher in some areas than in the example we give.)

RECOMMENDED SPENDING GUIDELINES

Estimate Your Expenses • Percentage Guide for Family Income

						$	%
Gross Income	$20,000	$30,000	$40,000	$50,000	$60,000	__	__
Giving	10%	10%	10%	10%	10%	__	__
Taxes and Social Security	17%	18%	19%	22%	22%	__	__
Net Spendable	$14,700	$21,500	$28,300	$33,700	$40,400	__	__
Housing	35%	35%	30%	29%	26%	__	__
Food	20%	16%	13%	11%	10%	__	__
Clothing	5%	5%	5%	4%	4%	__	__
Transportation	13%	10%	9%	8%	7%	__	__
Entertainment/Rec.	6%	7%	7%	8%	8%	__	__
Medical	3%	3%	3%	3%	3%	__	__
Insurance	2%	3%	3%	3%	3%	__	__
Children	3%	2%	2%	2%	2%	__	__
Gifts	2%	2%	2%	2%	2%	__	__
Miscellaneous	5%	5%	5%	5%	5%	__	__
Margin	5%	12%	21%	25%	30%	__	__

Assumptions for preceding table:

1. Figures are based on a family of four.
2. The tax deductions are giving, interest on home mortgage, and state, sales, and property taxes (average).
3. Home is owned.
4. There is no debt other than home mortgage.
5. All social security witholdings are from one wage earner.
6. The estimates are based on 1985 tax schedules and allowable deductions.
7. All living expenses are percentages of net spendable income.
8. Margin can be used for other expenses (debt, private education, savings, etc.).

> From *Master Your Money*. Ron Blue. Nashville, Tenn.:
> Thomas Nelson Publishers, 1985, 141.

REDUCING EXPENSES

If you've got some belt-tightening to do to get your finances in order, your efforts will need to be built on a regimen of controlling your expenses. You can take charge together by developing a plan, and then faithfully abiding by the rules you set forth in that plan.

In any partnership, one person is usually more gifted in the area of details and finances than the other. It is our recommendation that, as a couple, you capitalize on the gifts you've been given for the benefit of the partnership. There are some people who automatically believe that males have been given exclusive rights to money management by God himself. We would refer those people to Proverbs 31, where the ideal wife is making a bundle for her blessed husband and family! We have seen the greatest financial harmony in marriages where both husband and wife participate in the planning, the decision making, and the daily follow-through. Whatever works best and is most agreeable to you is the best plan to follow.

Financial predators enter the marriage as a result of either poor planning or failure to follow through. Here's a list of such predators:

1. Living beyond your means.
2. Increasing your expenses as income increases.
3. Hiding finances from your mate.
4. Micromanaging your mate's expenditures.
5. Living by the premise that "I shop, therefore I am."
6. Using credit cards as if they were cash.
7. Controlling your mate by humiliation when he or she needs money.
8. Living by the premise that "enough is never enough"; demanding more money, more earnings, more work, to get more things, more prestige, more power.

You can effectively overpower these predators by taking charge of this critical area of your marriage. It will take effort and time. There are no shortcuts to this one.

You can make a tremendous impact on reducing your expenses by first identifying areas where reductions can be made. Here are some specific, practical ways you can reduce your spending. We encourage you to jot down specific ideas you may have as you read through these items:

Housing. Housing and utilities may represent too large an expense each month. Would alternative living arrangements such as sharing a house, renting out a room, or moving to a smaller apartment be more advisable or economically feasible?

Food. If food represents a large monthly expenditure, a combination of brown-bagging lunch at work, eating more meals at home, sharing meals with family and friends, downgrading to less expensive meals or restaurants, shopping grocery store sales, and using coupons will help.

Clothing. Clothing costs can be reduced by "making do" with last year's fashions, repairing old clothing, dressing children in hand-me-downs, and shopping sales.

Telephone. It is worthwhile, from time to time, to reevaluate phone expenses. Are you paying monthly leasing fees? If so, can you reduce the number of phones you have? Would *buying* a phone be more economical? Is there a cheaper type of local service, such as measured service, that could satisfy your needs? Are you subscribing to features such as custom calling, call waiting, call forwarding, telephone answering, that you could do without (at least until bills are paid)? Have you selected a long-distance company that is tailored to your needs and calling patterns? Last but not least, making less frequent long-distance calls and reducing the length of those calls can produce big savings.

Credit cards. Pay off your credit cards, beginning with the ones with the highest interest. Plan how much extra you can pay each month on that particular card; meanwhile, continue to make payments on all cards. When one card is paid off, move to the next. Eventually, you will be free from credit card debt.

Get support. It may be helpful to you to inform friends and family that you are going through a difficult time financially. Ask them to rally around to help you in your efforts to get your financial house in order. Together, you can seek inexpensive forms of recreation: bargain movie matinees, museums, art galleries, jogging, nature hikes, hunting, fishing, swimming, reading, gardening, tennis, bicycling, free concerts, picnics, walks, playing board or yard games. Having fun does not depend on spending money.

Invite friends and family to join you. Consider it a contest to find the best deal on a prospective purchase or the most inexpensive form of entertainment. A competition among friends or family members in trying to locate that particular model refrigerator at the lowest price in town can be profitable and fun. Beating the crowds to drug and department stores for advertised specials, and using coupons once you get there, can help. You can become delighted with success at finding a bottle of shampoo on the shelf that is marked fifty cents less than other similar items. You can gloat over the fact that the jar of barbecue sauce you are using cost you a fraction of its usual cost. You will be amazed at the amount of money you can save in a month. Imagine the savings in a year!

Next, work out your budget. This will provide you with a point of reference. From this budget, you will be able to realistically look at your options for reducing expenses—*planning for the present and the future*. Then you can set out to develop a plan together. From there, the working of that plan—*the attending to the work*—will bring you to the goal of truly managing your money.

REDUCE EXPENSES STEP BY STEP

Step 1: Develop an income and expense sheet.

INCOME AND EXPENSE SHEET
Gross Income

Salary/wages	$_____
Investment income (dividends, etc.)	$_____
Social Security/disability	$_____
Interest income (savings, CDs, etc.)	$_____
Pensions and annuities	$_____
Alimony/child support	$_____
Unemployment	$_____
Other	$_____
Total gross income	$_____

Deductions from Gross Income

Taxes	$_____
Other	$_____
Total deductions	$_____

Available (Net) Income

Subtract applicable deductions from gross income	$_____

Expenses

Housing *(include insurance and taxes)*	$_____
Utilities	$_____
Household	$_____
Food	$_____
Transportation	$_____
Auto insurance	$_____
Life insurance	$_____
Children's expenses (recreation, lessons, etc.)	$_____
Clothing	$_____
Medical	$_____
Education	$_____
Savings	$_____
Charities	$_____
Church/tithe	$_____
Recreation	$_____
Gifts	$_____
Total expenses	$_____

Balance available, or cash flow

Subtract expenses from available income $_____

Step 2: Reduce expenses to increase cash flow, pay off debt, and live within your means.

Some simple mathematics can help here. Notice that saving $100 per month on any single expense will save you $1,200 per year. The small cutbacks add a great deal to cash flow over the course of a year. Here are a few examples:

Monthly Reduction————> Annual Reduction	
$10	$120
$20	$240
$50	$600
$100	$1,200
$250	$3,000
$500	$6,000
$1,000	12,000

Any reduction you can make from monthly expenses will have a bearing on reducing debt and increasing cash flow. Review your expenses with your spouse and look for possible ways to cut down. This may involve selling some assets so that you can apply the money from those sales to your expenses, thereby reducing your debt. The more conscious you both are of how quickly a few dollars here and a few dollars there can add up, the greater commitment you will make to working within a budget.

There are numerous complexities to financial planning. The purpose of this presentation is to help you get started. Money is an important area, well worth your time and effort. We highly recommend you add to your knowledge and skills in the area of personal finance. Excellent and comprehensive resources are available. See the "Money Matters" division under "Recommended Reading" for resources which combine biblical guidelines with good business practices.

∾

How Do We Set Goals for Our Marriage?

Here's a list of areas you will want to include as you contemplate your goals for marriage. They are areas that impact our lives so strongly that they may lead to the success or failure of your marriage:

1. Family finances
2. Communications
3. Division of labor
4. Child-rearing
5. Recreation
6. Romance
7. Pursuit of friendships
8. Spiritual growth
9. Future planning, long-term and short-term
10. Career planning
11. Personal needs
12. Hobbies
13. Quiet time
14. Ministry
15. Scheduling
16. Sex life
17. Physical fitness
18. Nutrition
19. Health
20. Education
21. Marriage maintenance

22. Extended family relationships
23. Holidays and special events
24. Housing and lifestyle

The above list is not exhaustive. You may have some other topics to include that are more important to your personal situation. Please modify the list to cover those bases. Once you have modified the list, you will be ready to proceed to the assignments below.

Assignment 1

Purchase one notebook for each of you. Now, look over the list of twenty-four items. Each of you privately write down your personal goals for each item. Let us suggest that you write your individual goals from the first-person point-of-view: "I want our marriage to be free from unnecessary debt."

Perhaps you feel inept at managing money and your spouse has excellent skills in this area. For you, it would be wise to delegate the management of finances to your spouse. However, we recommend that you discuss matters thoroughly, agree on financial decisions, and never use money to control your mate.

We also recommend you put together a thorough budget, and stick to that budget as dedicated business partners. This part of marriage is like a small business. Couples find it helpful to use ledgers or computer software, and keep receipts and records for tax preparation. Excellent books and resources are available to teach you how; they even provide forms and examples to guide you (see the "Money Matters" division under "Recommended Reading").

Assignment 2

Step 1: Share your reasons for writing your goals as stated (in Assignment 1). In this example, one spouse may want to have the resources to give more freely to certain charitable organizations.

Step 2: If your goals conflict, try to strike a compromise and write down a joint goal. If this is successful, you have developed a common goal.

Step 3 If no compromise can be reached, negotiate a completely new option or game plan. This might include talking to a financial manager, consulting written resources, or comparing notes with other couples.

In this example, a wise new plan might be for the husband to simply give what he can cheerfully give, and be glad to see his wife giving according to her convictions out of the income that she brings to the marriage.

Proceed through your list of goals. It may take a number of weeks before you are satisfied that you have a workable plan. Think of it as a painting of the wonderful marriage you dreamed you could build. This plan will provide satisfaction and substance to your expectations. The time you commit to it will tend to reduce conflict, disappointment, and feelings of hurt or resentment. It is truly a conflict-preventing program. Once you get the hang of it, the process can be enjoyable as well.

Assignment 3

You began, in Assignment 1, by writing goals from a personal, "I" point of view. In Assignment 2 you discussed your personal goals, and tried to agree on joint goals.

Now you will record the joint goals you agreed on in Assignment 2. Please write your joint goals from the "we" point of view. For example, "We will...." "We agree to...." Do this for each item on your list of goals.

Assignment 4

Some goals are by nature more important than others. List your goals in order of priority. Make your spiritual goals number one, and proceed from there. Here is an example of the beginning of a prioritized list of goals:

1. *Spiritual growth.* We want to make God first in our own lives and in our marriage. We want to demonstrate his preeminence in our lives by setting aside time for personal and mutual worship and prayer. We will seek the fellowship of other believers and raise our children to love and serve God. We will consider the needs of our friends and neighbors and take opportunities to give to and help others. We will take the time to grow in our knowledge of God and his will for our lives.

2. *Communication.* We desire to take time daily to talk about the experiences of our day. We will talk about our victories and our disappointments, and will encourage each other to make good choices. We will allow for complaints, some whining and venting, as well as the nitty-gritty details of what is important to our mate. We will make every effort to include good news that will uplift and encourage our mate. We will share pain and disappointment so that we can pray for, uphold, and encourage each other. We are committed to being a team and to staying in tune with each other. We will make every effort to give the best we have to give, not the leftovers, in this important area.

3. *Romance.* We will keep our romance vital and fresh. We will try to keep our spirit of courtship alive in the marriage. We will date at least twice a month. We will take private time away from kids, family, and friends to talk and have fun doing things in the home and away from home. These private times could include: candlelight dinners, romantic restaurants and settings, walks on the beach at sunset, picnics in the park, and musical events. We will hold hands, find out-of-the-way places, hold each other, sit closely, and kiss affectionately. (Refer to chapter eight, "Keeping Romance Alive.")

We have offered these three examples as a "starter kit." This exercise is highly personal. Your goals will be custom-made!

Assignment 5

Develop an action plan for each of the listed goals. Be very specific. For example, set dates, times, activities, and places to achieve your goals. The more specific you make the action plan, the more likely it is that you will actually do it. We expect you will find this exercise very enriching and enjoyable.

One man, whom Gary had required to work through these assignments with his wife-to-be, told Gary that, six months into their marriage, he sensed something was wrong. He reviewed the goals he and his wife had agreed on, only to discover that he was not doing his part. For one thing, his job had become all too important and had eaten away at their communication time. He was getting home in time to eat dinner alone and go to bed. He made the necessary adjustments and thanked Gary for requiring them to write out their goals.

Goal-setting is designed to help you bring good ideas to the table, negotiate even better ideas, and then to live those ideas. Keep your goals and objectives in a location where you can review them occasionally. Certain goals will need modification now and then. Others will remain the same. Reviewing the goals will give you an opportunity to evaluate your progress.

RECOMMENDED READING
∽

ADDICTION

Carnes, Patrick. *Out of the Shadows: Understanding Sexual Addiction.* Minneapolis: CompCare, 1985.

Covington, Stephanie, and Liana Beckett. *Leaving the Enchanted Forest: The Path from Relationship Addiction to Intimacy.* San Francisco: HarperSan Francisco, 1988.

Life Recovery Bible, the Living Bible. Wheaton, Illinois: Tyndale, 1992.

Nakken, Craig. *The Addictive Personality: Understanding Compulsion in Our Lives.* New York: Harper/Hazeldon, 1988.

The Twelve Steps of Alcoholics Anonymous: Interpreted by the Hazeldon Foundation. New York: Harper/Hazeldon.

BOUNDARIES, CONTROLLING BEHAVIOR, RECOVERY

Batemen, Linda L. *Bible Promises for the Healing Journey.* Westwood, N.J.: Barbour, 1989.

Beattie, Melody. *The Language of Letting Go.* New York: Harper Collins, 1990.

Bower, Sharon Anthony and Gordon H. *Asserting Yourself: A Practical Guide for Positive Change.* Reading, Mass.: Addison-Wesley, 1991.

Bradshaw, John. *Healing the Shame that Binds You.* Deerfield Beach, Fla.: Health Communications, 1988.

Buehler, Rich. *New Choices, New Boundaries.* Nashville: Nelson, 1991.

Cloud, Henry, and John Townsend. *Boundaries.* Grand Rapids, Mich.: Zondervan, 1992.

Mellody, Pia, and Andrea Wells Miller and J. Keith Miller. *Facing Codependence: What It Is, Where It Comes from and How It Sabotages Our Lives.* San Francisco: HarperSan Francisco, 1989.

Townsend, John. *Hiding from Love.* Colorado Springs: NavPress, 1992.

FAMILY OF ORIGIN AND HEALING FROM PAST HURTS

Carder, Dave, and Earl Henslin, John Townsend, Henry Cloud, and Alice Brawand. *Secrets of Your Family Tree: Healing for Adult Children of Dysfunctional Families.* Chicago: Moody, 1991.

Feldmeth, Joanne Ross, and Midge Wallace Finley. *We Weep for Ourselves and Our Children: A Christian Guide for Survivors of Childhood Sexual Abuse.* San Francisco: HarperSan Francisco, 1990.

Frank, Jan. *A Door of Hope: Recognizing and Resolving the Pains of Your Past.* Nashville: Nelson, 1993.

Seamands, David A. *Putting Away Childish Things.* Wheaton, Ill.: Victor, 1986.

Stanley, Charles. *The Gift of Forgiveness.* Nashville: Nelson, 1991.

Thurman, Chris. *The Lies We Believe.* Nashville: Nelson, 1989.

The Twelve Steps, A Spiritual Journey by Friends in Recovery. San Diego: RPI, 1994.

Wilson, Sandra D. *Hurt People Hurt People.* Nashville: Nelson, 1993.

MONEY MATTERS

Blue, Ron. *Master Your Money: A Step-By-Step Plan for Financial Freedom.* Nashville: Nelson, 1986.

Blue, Ron. *Taming the Money Master.* Colorado Springs: Focus on the Family, 1993.

Burkett, Larry. *Answers to Your Family's Financial Problems.* Colorado Springs: Focus on the Family, 1987.

Burkett, Larry. *How to Manage Your Money.* Chicago: Moody, 1975.

Burkett, Larry. *Use Your Money Wisely.* Chicago: Moody, 1985.

SEXUALITY

Kaplan, Helen Singer. *The New Sex Therapy.* New York: Brunner/Mazel, 1974. This excellent work was written for therapists. It combines scientific medical information, psychology, and actual therapeutic treatment of sexual dysfunction. This is a comprehensive source book written in a professional medical and psychotherapy style.

Penner, Clifford and Joyce. *Have Fun, Fantastic Sex: A Guidebook for Married Couples.* Nashville: Nelson, 1994. This is a resource book for couples to enhance their lovemaking repertoire.

Penner, Clifford and Joyce. *The Gift of Sex: A Guide to Sexual Fulfillment.* Dallas: Word, 1981. This book offers many practical ideas and excellent comprehensive information about sexual fulfillment from a Christian viewpoint. This book was written in everyday language for couples.

Wright, H. Norman, and Clifford and Joyce Penner. *In Touch with Each Other: A Couples' Guide to Marital Communication.* Elgin, Ill.: David C. Cook, 1976. This is a guide for couples to use to enhance communication and resolve conflict for the sexual fulfillment in their marriage.